The
UNFOLDING OF
GOD'S WORK
IN THE
LAST DAYS

GREGORY RANGER

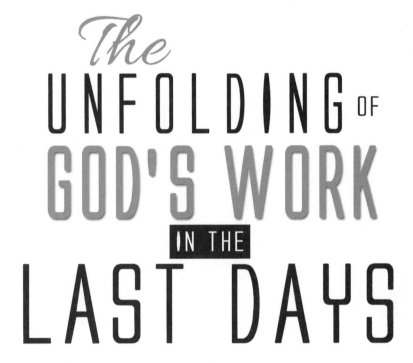

The
UNFOLDING OF
GOD'S WORK
IN THE
LAST DAYS

PREPARE TO RECEIVE OUR KING

CFI
An Imprint of Cedar Fort, Inc.
Springville, Utah

ISBN 13: 978-1-4621-1823-6

Published by CFI, an imprint of Cedar Fort, Inc.
2373 W. 700 S., Springville, UT 84663
Distributed by Cedar Fort, Inc., www.cedarfort.com

LIBRARY OF CONGRESS CATALOGING-IN-PUBLICATION DATA

Names: Ranger, Gregory, 1959- author.
Title: The unfolding of God's work in the last days / Gregory Ranger.
Description: Springville, Utah : CFI, an imprint of Cedar Fort, Inc., [2016]
  | "2016 | Includes bibliographical references and index.
Identifiers: LCCN 2016007884 (print) | LCCN 2016009727 (ebook) | ISBN
  9781462118236 (perfect bound : alk. paper) | ISBN 9781462126262 (epub,
  pdf, mobi)
Subjects: LCSH: End of the world. | Church of Jesus Christ of Latter-day
  Saints--Doctrines. | Mormon Church--Doctrines.
Classification: LCC BX8643.E83 R36 2016 (print) | LCC BX8643.E83 (ebook) |
  DDC 236/.9--dc23
LC record available at http://lccn.loc.gov/2016007884

Cover design by Shawnda T. Craig
Cover design © 2016 Cedar Fort, Inc.
Edited and typeset by Kevin Haws

Printed in the United States of America

10 9 8 7 6 5 4 3 2 1

Printed on acid-free paper

To Dawn, Jonathan, Jessica, Jason, Jenna, Jaira, and Jaden

CONTENTS

ACKNOWLEDGMENTS

I *would like* to thank the following individuals: Brad Ranger, David Richards, and Hyrum Tynan for their valuable input; Mark Evans and Allan Fletcher for their suggestions and comments on content; the staff at Cedar Fort for their great support, awesome designs, and invaluable assistance in editing; and my dear wife, Dawn, for her support and encouragement during the long hours of research and writing.

PREFACE

Writing the Book

While *searching out* answers to gospel questions with a friend of mine, I had the opportunity to discuss some of my thoughts with a couple of well-established authors in the Church. Their comments made me realize that I had something positive to contribute and that the study of time and sequence had yet to be researched in depth.

One day, my friend said, "I think you should write a book. There are people who need to understand this information. They will want to know." I expressed the concern that maybe there would not be enough content to merit writing a book. He responded, "You're not done studying yet, are you? Don't worry, the rest will come." And so it began.

Book Style

In an effort to create a more efficient reference book, I have incorporated various methods of presenting information. Many scriptures use italicized words for emphasis. This is ongoing throughout the book. All such occurrences are "emphasis added." Occasionally, you will also notice that there are lengthy quotations. The purpose is to allow readers to enjoy the full quotation, as it is pertinent and informative and eliminates the inconvenience of searching out the quote. This can be especially helpful for those who have limited access or research ability.

For the purpose of convenience, I have tried to include the appropriate amount of scriptures to provide context and clarity for readers. This also allows readers to enjoy the book without having to search out scriptural references. At the end of each chapter, I have included summary points.

Why This Book Is Important

Without a clear understanding of the path ahead, it can be difficult to have direction in our lives. We live in a time when there are many voices telling us how to live, what we should or should not do, and what we should believe in. A firm understanding of the unfolding of God's works in the last days will help us to proceed with confidence. God is not the author of confusion, and He has given us direction in the scriptures. He wants us to understand this information, to follow our leaders, and to seek for His help so that He may direct us in our earthly missions.

Responsibility for This Text

If there are any faults with the interpretation of the scriptures, I alone am to blame. In areas where suggestions are made or opinions are expressed, they are my own and should in no way be taken as doctrinal or authoritative. Though I am a seeker of truth, I offer up no claims that this information is absolute truth. I will be the first to welcome any information that sheds further light on the contents of this book.

My hope is that by sharing this, I can begin to fulfill my responsibility as a member of the kingdom, as found in the Doctrine and Covenants 88:77–80:

And I give unto you a commandment that you shall teach one another the doctrine of the kingdom . . . that you may be instructed more perfectly . . . of things both in heaven and in the earth, and under the earth; things which have been, things which are, things which must shortly come to pass; things which are at home, things which are abroad; the wars and the perplexities of the nations, and the judgments which are on the land; and a knowledge also of countries and of kingdoms . . . that ye may be prepared in all things.

INTRODUCTION

"And then shall my revelations which I have caused to
be written by my servant John be unfolded in the eyes
of all the people. Remember, when ye see these things,
ye shall know that the time is at hand that they shall
be made manifest in very deed." (Ether 4:16)

The time and sequence of signs and events leading up to
the Second Coming of Christ has been, for many, an area
of uncertainty and speculation. Whether revelation comes
by prophecy, visions, dreams, or near-death experiences, it does not
come with dates and times for indexing purposes. As people continue to receive warnings and to prepare for the last days, many feel
that there is no certain way to know how or when or in what order
these events will unfold.

Until now, the focus by scholars on the book of Revelation has
been, for the most part, a detailed analysis of symbolism. As these
revelations begin to unfold, it is essential for all who live in this time
to have a clearer understanding of these events and the purposes of

God as His work continues to roll forth. The Lord desires for His Saints to have an understanding of how the work is to unfold.

Through His prophets, the Lord has given us the signs and information necessary to understand the events that will take place prior to His Second Coming. Like the Wise Men of old, we must seek to understand these revelations in order to be properly prepared.

A closer examination of the scriptures, using the perspective of time and sequence, will increase our understanding and give greater context to the words of the prophets. We will be able to more fully understand the signs and events of the last days. As these events and their time sequences are more clearly identified, reason and structure will transform our perception of when and how God's work is to unfold.

For example, the scriptures tell us that there will be at least two earthquakes of worldwide proportions prior to the Lord's coming—one in the sixth seal (Revelation 6:12–14; D&C 88:89–91) and one in the seventh seal (Revelation 11:19; 16:18–20; D&C 133:44). For those who have read but do not understand, the first earthquake of this magnitude could easily be mistaken for the earthquake that directly precedes the coming of Christ. What are the consequences of such an event? How will this impact the world and our faith? How much time is there between these earthquakes?

In a world where the political, economic, and moral landscapes are in a state of constant change, life is unsettling. It is difficult to see the bigger picture. While the wars and economic crisis that we experience in today's world are devastating, these events will not be the trigger to cause the worldwide change that will precede the Second Coming of Jesus Christ.

If we examine the scriptures, we will see that there are certain specific events that will change our world. These are the events the Lord has identified as signs to watch for as He begins to prepare the earth for His return.

There is a message in the increased calamities that are coming upon us. While our preparations against war and economic distress are surely beneficial, our preparations should be focused on a much greater calamity that will undoubtedly come upon us.

The focus of this book is to identify, clarify, and expound upon certain events and conditions that are to transpire in the last days and put them into their time and sequence. Through the perspective of time and sequence, we will get a clearer picture of where in the timeline these events are to take place and allow for a better understanding of the events themselves.

The Lord has told us that there are seven seals that represent the earth's temporal existence. Where are we in this process? How accurate are our calculations of the timeline between Adam and the present day? In which of the seven seals do we live? We have also been told that the Lord will shorten the days. When might this happen? How does this affect our calculations? The scriptures provide the much-needed insight into these questions.

How far away is the Second Coming? We know neither the hour nor the day—not even the angels in heaven know. The Lord has given us time indicators so that we can watch the signs and thereby know the approximate timeframes. The nearer we are to the Second Coming, the more relevant this information will become.

As we take the time to understand what the Lord has already revealed, we can prepare for the future with greater purpose and an increased comprehension of the path ahead.

Our review of the scriptures, for the most part, will not include a detailed analysis of symbolism; instead, we will take a more practical approach to understand the messages that are being communicated.

> Wherefore I shall prophesy according to the plainness which hath been with me from the time that I came out from Jerusalem with my father; for behold, my soul delighteth in plainness unto my people, that they may learn. (2 Nephi 25:4)

Nephi teaches us that a plain message is more profitable for learning; therefore, in some cases, a verse or a chapter will be quoted and then be given a plain interpretation. By analyzing a passage of scripture in this manner, we will be enabled to see through any extraneous details.

The scriptural accounts of these events only touch on some of the events that will transpire in the last days. There are many wars and rumors of wars, plagues, economic and political upheavals, invasions, and sins of every kind that are not referenced. That is why it is important to identify specific events that are to take place and separate them out from the many events that are taking place—and will continue to take place. By isolating certain specific events, we will be able to follow the unfolding of God's work, as documented in the scriptures.

As we examine the scriptures, many stumbling blocks stand in the way of acquiring knowledge. We need to be aware of these obstacles and prepare ourselves to learn. In Timothy, we read,

> This know also, that *in the last days perilous times shall come.*
>
> For *men shall be lovers of their own selves*, covetous, boasters, *proud*, blasphemers, disobedient to parents, unthankful, *unholy*,
>
> Without natural affection, trucebreakers, false accusers, incontinent, fierce, despisers of those that are good,
>
> Traitors, heady, highminded, *lovers of pleasures more than lovers of God*;
>
> Having a form of godliness, but denying the power thereof: from such turn away. . . .
>
> *Ever learning, and never able to come to the knowledge of the truth.*
> (2 Timothy 3:1–5, 7)

First, we need to unburden ourselves from the world. We cannot be lovers of pleasures more than lovers of God. We must have more than a form of godliness. When we are free from the world, we can hear the whisperings of the Spirit. If we do not overcome this part of the process, we will continue to spin our wheels and, as it states in verse seven, we will be "ever learning, and never able to come to the knowledge of the truth."

The scriptures tell us of the efforts that are required to learn and that not all things are easily understood.

> Wherefore, hearken, *O my people*, which are of the house of Israel, and give ear unto my words; for because *the words of Isaiah are not plain unto you*, nevertheless *they are plain unto all those that are filled with the spirit of prophecy*. (2 Nephi 25:4)

The process of examining the scriptures, according to the spirit of prophecy, requires faith, obedience, sanctification, and sincere effort for divine assistance. We must be willing to take the time to seek the Lord's help and become engaged in the learning process. Information can elude us if we do not seek for it, or if we lack real intent:

> Behold, you have not understood; you have supposed that I would give it unto you, when you took no thought save it was to ask me. (D&C 9:7)

> And if ye *shall ask with a sincere heart, with real intent, having faith in Christ, he will manifest the truth of it unto you, by the power of the Holy Ghost.* (Moroni 10:4)

We must analyze the information and be open to the promptings of the Spirit. Light can be shed on the thoughts and writings of the prophets when we follow this process.

Two Book of Mormon prophets—Jacob and Alma—give us the following admonition:

> *Arouse the faculties of your souls*; shake yourselves that ye may awake from the slumber of death. (Jacob 3:11)

> *Awake and arouse your faculties.* (Alma 32:27)

To arouse our faculties, we must acquire a heightened sense of purpose. We must study in earnest, with specific goals or questions. To awake, we must awaken unto the light and life that comes from God—meaning the Spirit. This process of awakening and arousing our faculties allows us to search the scriptures using the light of the Holy Spirit to find gospel truths.

By identifying gospel truths, we will not be swayed by every wind of doctrine. As we approach the Second Coming of Jesus Christ, our journey will have uncertainties. There will be those who have visions or dreams or revelations—good people who will warn their neighbors. There will also be many soothsayers and predictors, crying lo here and there.

And then if any man shall say to you, *Lo, here is Christ; or, lo, he is there; believe him not:*

For *false Christs and false prophets shall rise*, and shall shew signs and wonders, to seduce, if it were possible, even the elect.

But take *ye heed*: behold, *I have foretold you all things.* (Mark 13:21–23)

Here, the Lord also indicates that the answers are in the scriptures. Because people do not seek answers in the scriptures, they are confused about the timing and signs. Such will think that the Second Coming is upon us, when in fact the time will not have arrived. Many will lose hope that the Lord will ever come:

And they shall say that Christ delayeth his coming until the end of the earth. (D&C 45:26)

A sound understanding of the time and sequence of the events of the last days will help us to better prepare and give us the quiet assurance that comes from the Spirit once we have been enlightened.

Knowledge changes our patterns of thought and, subsequently, our actions. Many battles have been won using critical information like the enemy's movements or battle plan. Understanding how God's work is to unfold will allow us to be better prepared for these events and follow them with certainty as they happen around and to us. It will assist us in making choices that will affect our lives and the lives of others.

As individuals, families, and communities, we must be prepared. The Nephites had to make preparations to defend themselves against the Lamanites. Noah had to build an ark to prepare for the flood. We have been warned to make preparations. Men will think that they are prepared, but in reality they will not be.

But verily, thus saith the Lord, let not your flight be in haste, but let all things be prepared before you; and he that goeth, let him not look back lest sudden destruction shall come upon him. (D&C 133:15)

This warning from the Doctrine and Covenants refers to more than spiritual preparedness. The main focus of the Brethren of the

Church has always been and will always be to cry repentance. However, in addition to crying repentance, they bring warnings from the Lord. Being spiritually prepared is only part of the formula. Warnings like this are straight to the point:

> The revelation to produce and store food may be as essential to our temporal welfare today as boarding the ark was to the people in the days of Noah. (Ezra Taft Benson, "To the Fathers in Israel," *Ensign*, November 1980)

These warnings, which continue from time to time, can help us become like the five wise virgins. As conditions in the world continue to erode, we will see the wisdom of being physically and spiritually prepared. As individuals, it is our responsibility to be prepared. How many years did Noah preach repentance unto the people before the floods came?

May those who read this book gain an increased understanding of how events in the last days will unfold and find the wisdom to heed prophetic warnings and make the necessary preparations to assist themselves and their loved ones as time of the Second Coming approaches.

> And though the heavens and the earth pass away, my word shall not pass away, but shall all be fulfilled, whether by mine own voice or by the voice of my servants, it is the same. (D&C 1:38)

CHAPTER 1: TIME PARAMETERS

As we examine the signs and events of the last days, there are some critical observations that will give us a better understanding of the function of time and the key role it plays in revealing a greater knowledge of how God's work will unfold. The Lord, through His prophets, has given us a guide in the form of the scriptures to help us understand the last days.

The Apostle John was given the task of writing the largest compilation of revelatory information comprising details of the signs and events of the last days.

> And then shall *my revelations which I have caused to be written by my servant John* be unfolded in the eyes of all the people. Remember, when ye see these things, ye shall know that the time is at hand that they shall be made manifest in very deed. (Ether 4:16)

This scripture confirms the importance of the book of Revelation as the reference point for all other prophecies concerning the last days so as to establish time and sequence. John records events as they transpire, according to seals, or time periods.

And I saw in the right hand of him that sat on the throne a book written within and on the backside, *sealed with seven seals*. (Revelation 5:1)

When the Prophet Joseph inquired of the Lord on the subject, he was given this answer:

Q. What are we to understand by the book which John saw, which was sealed on the back with seven seals?
A. We are to understand that it contains the revealed will, mysteries, and the works of God; the hidden things of his economy concerning this earth during the seven thousand years of its continuance, or its temporal existence. (D&C 77:6)

As a further explanation about these seven seals, the Lord has revealed,

Q. What are we to understand by the seven seals with which it was sealed?
A. We are to understand that *the first seal contains the things of the first thousand years, and the second also of the second thousand years,* and so on until the seventh. (D&C 77:7)

The Lord explains that the things of each seal belong to that seal. He also states that each seal is for a different and sequential thousand-year period. Finally, He uses a certain manner of language that indicates one seal is finished before the next seal is opened:

When he had opened the second seal. . . .
When he had opened the third seal. . . .
When he had opened the fourth seal. . . . (Revelation 6:3, 5, 7)

All of these things point to the conclusion that the seals themselves are independent from one another. We can look toward each seal and its events in a sequential manner. In this way. we will not think an event has happened when it is yet to come.

Throughout the scriptures, it is said that God's course is one eternal round; His house is a house of order; there is no deviating to the left or to the right; His word is light and truth; He is a God of truth; He is the same yesterday, today, and forever; and there is no reason to doubt His word.

The Lord is not an author of confusion, nor does He walk in crooked paths. In our day, we experience much confusion, whether in our own lives or in the affairs of the nations in which we live. Even though the geological and meteorological events that are coming to pass in our day seem to be ever-increasing and chaotic, it does not mean that the times and the revolutions of the planets are not in a set plan and that the creations of our Father are not subject to His command.

Time and the Seven Seals

From the interpretation given to Joseph Smith about the book that was sealed with seven seals, we understand that the earth has a set time for its temporal existence: seven thousand years. We also understand that the temporal existence of the earth is divided into seven distinct periods, or seals of a thousand years. As we read the scriptures, it is difficult to reconcile the time allotted in the seventh seal with the time required for the events that are prophesied to take place.

How is it possible that, in the beginning of the seventh seal, the Lord will prepare the earth for His coming, reign personally upon the earth for a thousand years, and then release Satan for a brief period of time, all within the thousand years of the seventh seal? At first glance, this seems mathematically impossible. Let us review the scriptures that outline these events.

In the beginning of the seventh seal prior to His return, the Lord will prepare the earth:

Q. What are we to understand by the sounding of the trumpets, mentioned in the 8th chapter of Revelation?

A. We are to understand that as God made the world in six days, and on the seventh day he finished his work, and sanctified it, and also formed man out of the dust of the earth, even so, *in the beginning of the seventh thousand years will the Lord God sanctify the earth, and complete the salvation of man,* and judge all things, and shall redeem all things, except that which he hath not put into his power, when he shall have sealed all things, unto the end of all things; and the sounding of the trumpets of the seven angels are the preparing and finishing of his work, *in the beginning of the seventh thousand years— the preparing of the way before the time of his coming.* (D&C 77:12)

The scriptures are quite clear in indicating that this preparation will take place prior to the time of His coming. This period of preparation will include an opportunity for the 144,000 to go forth upon the earth in one last effort to find the elect who will come to Zion. It will also be a time of testing or purification for the Saints. And during this time, we will see the final uprising of wickedness, as the forces of the adversary will have all power. It is in this time when the ends of justice will be satisfied in fulfilling the command of the Almighty to reap the earth.

After these events are completed, the Lord will then reign upon the earth for a thousand years.

And it came to pass that Enoch saw the day of the *coming of the Son of Man, in the last days, to dwell on the earth in righteousness for the space of a thousand years.* (Moses 7:65)

It is important to note that only after His coming will the Lord dwell on the earth. We must remember that He is a resurrected being, and the earth must be prepared for Him to reside on it.

Finally, the earth will be spared for a little season.

And again, verily, verily, I say unto you that *when the thousand years are ended,* and men again begin to deny their God, *then will I spare the earth but for a little season;*

And the end shall come, and the heaven and the earth shall be consumed and pass away, and there shall be a new heaven and a new earth. (D&C 29:22–23)

And so on, until the seventh angel shall sound his trump; and he shall stand forth upon the land and upon the sea, and swear in the name of him who sitteth upon the throne, that there shall be time no longer; and Satan shall be bound, that old serpent, who is called *the devil, and shall not be loosed for the space of a thousand years.*

And *then he shall be loosed for a little season*, that he may gather together his armies.

And Michael, the seventh angel, even the archangel, shall gather together his armies, even the hosts of heaven.

And the devil shall gather together his armies; even the hosts of hell, and shall come up to battle against Michael and his armies.

And then cometh the battle of the great God; *and the devil and his armies shall be cast away into their own place, that they shall not have power over the saints any more at all.* (D&C 88:110–14)

If we include the periods prior to and after the thousand-year reign of Christ, it is evident that these events add up to more than one thousand years. The scriptures also inform us that all of these events are to take place during the seventh seal.

This has created some confusion for those who read the scriptures. Many simply consider it to be part of the mysteries of God.

Instead of searching for the answer to the "time problem," some have tried to find alternate ways to make the information fit as it should. The difficulty with this type of thinking is that we are forced to compromise the meaning of the scriptures by finding some convoluted interpretation to make sense of the information.

Examining the facts, we know that the Lord will reign personally upon the earth for a thousand years, and during this same time Satan will be bound for a thousand years.

And he laid hold on the dragon, that old serpent, which is the Devil, and Satan, and *bound him a thousand years.* (Revelation 20:2)

The question to be answered is this: Why is the duration of the seventh seal longer than a thousand earth years? If we examine additional information about *time* in the scriptures, we can see that what the prophets were describing is indeed accurate—the seventh seal is in fact longer than a thousand earth years. There are just a few more pieces of the puzzle to be considered.

From the Pearl of Great Price, we understand that the revolutions of the planets and their placement in the galaxy have an effect on time, relative to Kolob at the center, and revolutions of planets in the same region of space can have different set times.

> And the Lord said unto me, by the Urim and Thummim, that *Kolob* was after the manner of the Lord, according to its times and seasons in the revolutions thereof; that *one revolution was a day unto the Lord,* after his manner of reckoning, *it being one thousand years according to the time appointed unto that whereon thou standest.* This is *the reckoning of the Lord's time, according to the reckoning of Kolob.*
>
> And the Lord said unto me: The planet which is the lesser light, lesser than that which is to rule the day, even the night, is above or greater than that upon which thou standest in point of reckoning, *for it moveth in order more slow*; this is in order because it standeth above the earth upon which thou standest, *therefore the reckoning of its time is not so many as to its number of days, and of months, and of years.* (Abraham 3:4–5)

Thus we see that the contrary must also true—when the number of days, months, and years are shorter, the planet is moving faster.

> And the Lord said unto me: Now, Abraham, these two facts exist, behold thine eyes see it; it is given unto thee to know the times of reckoning, and the set time, yea, the set time of the earth upon which thou standest, and the set time of the greater light which is set to rule the day, and the set time of the lesser light which is set to rule the night.
>
> Now the set time of the lesser light is a longer time as to its reckoning than the reckoning of the time of the earth upon which thou standest.
>
> And where these two facts exist, there shall be another fact above them, that is, there shall be another planet whose reckoning of time shall be longer still;
>
> And thus *there shall be the reckoning of the time of one planet above another, until thou come nigh unto Kolob,* which Kolob is after the reckoning of the Lord's time; which *Kolob is set nigh unto the throne of God, to govern all those planets which belong to the same order as that upon which thou standest.* (Abraham 3:6–9)

At the time when this revelation was given to Abraham, the reckoning of time was one day on Kolob was equal to one thousand years on earth. Knowing that time is reckoned according to Kolob, it would seem logical that the length of the each seal is actually equal to one day on Kolob, and the temporal existence of the earth is equal to seven days on Kolob. Because we know that the Lord controls the reckoning of time for His creations, it is also understandable that the Lord can change the reckoning of time.

In referring to the reckoning of time in our day, the Lord does say that on this earth, the days will be shortened.

> And except that the Lord had shortened those days, no flesh should be saved: but for the elect's sake, whom he hath chosen, *he hath shortened the days*. (Mark 13:20)

To illustrate the effect of increasing the speed of the earth's rotation even slightly, consider this: an increase of half a second per minute would result in a daily deficit of twelve minutes; in the course of a year, that would be the equivalent of three days; over the span of a thousand years, that would total three thousand days, or a little over eight years. It should also be noted that for the years to be shortened, the time required for the earth to orbit the sun would also have to be changed. While discussing planets of a different order, the Lord indicated that the days, months, and years were affected.

The consequence of this information is that once the Lord has shortened the days, it will then be possible to have one thousand and thirty, one thousand and fifty, or even one thousand and one hundred years be equal to a normal one thousand years of time, as reckoned on earth in the days of Abraham.

This information could also have implications on the other seals, as we do not know at what point the Lord will shorten the days. Using this knowledge, we can see how it is possible that the length of the seventh seal will be longer than a thousand earth years. This is how the Lord can prepare the earth for His coming, reign personally upon the earth for a thousand earth years, and then release Satan for a short season—all during the seventh seal.

Given that the Lord will at some point change the time of the days on earth, when it occurs the earth will no longer be in the same sequence with Kolob, as it was in the days of Abraham. Perhaps the Lord will shorten the days or change the set time of the earth when the worldwide earthquake happens in the sixth seal—when the mountains and islands are moved out of their place, and the earth reels to and fro like a drunken man.

We are not privy to the comings and the goings of the Lord when it comes to the reckoning of time. And even if we did have an accurate accounting of the years between Adam and the present (which we do not), it would still be difficult to accurately determine the beginning and the end of the various seals. We are therefore required, as them of old, to watch for the signs and live by faith. This is why even the angels know neither the day nor the hour when the Savior will come again.

Adam to the Present Day

As we examine the time frames for our day, there are several questions that are often the subject of discussion and debate. How long has it been since Adam and Eve began mortal existence? Is there an accurate calculation of this time period? Is there any reason to believe that this information belongs to us people? How many years after Adam was Christ born? In which seal was Christ born? Are we in the sixth seal, or are we in the seventh seal?

The genealogy of the Bible, up to and including the life of Noah, is confirmed in *Lectures on Faith*. The time period between the flood and Jesus Christ is somewhat generalized at best. Scholars have not found any scriptural or revelatory information I am aware of that would indicate an exact time. The Doctrine and Covenants states the following:

> The rise of the Church of Christ in these last days, being one thousand eight hundred and thirty years since the coming of our Lord and Savior Jesus Christ in the flesh, it being regularly organized and established agreeable to the laws of our country, by the will and

commandments of God, in the fourth month, and on the sixth day
of the month which is called April. (D&C 20:1)

As this verse was not part of the original text but was actually
added later—as an edit performing an informational function—it
is not revelatory but rather a manner of speech. There is not enough
information to accurately establish the period between Noah and
Christ.

The Bible has a genealogical record of births and deaths. Though
this information itself may be accurate, it does not allow us to make
precise calculations. The biblical information, though recorded in
years, does not allow us to calculate the days and months to establish proper timelines. For example, when Adam was 130 years old,
he begat Seth. Now, was Seth born 6 days after Adam turned 130
years old, or was he born 11 months and 6 days after? There is a
difference of eleven months. This information is not 100 percent
accurate, especially when you add up all the generations between
Adam and Christ.

If all the years of biblical history are added up between Adam
and Christ, the number of years does not equal four thousand.
Biblical scholars are not in agreement on exactly how many years
fewer than that would be accurate. Attempts to establish times and
dates would be, for the most part, educated guesses. Some histori-
ans speculate that as many as eighty years may be needed to bridge
the gap. Others believe it is closer to thirty.

The majority of the confusion centers on the reign of the kings.
During this time period, respected scholars can vary twenty or thirty
years in their calculations, depending on the suppositions that they
make when calculating.

Many simply assume that Christ was born four thousand years
after Adam, representing the beginning of the fifth seal, or a new time
in the history of the earth. As we examine the information that we
have available in the scriptures, we see the following:

And when he had opened the fifth seal, I saw under the altar the souls
of them that were slain for the word of God, and for the testimony
which they held. (Revelation 6:9)

We can suppose that this refers to the Saints who were so severely persecuted during the rise of Christianity, after the death of Christ, as this fits with an approximate time frame.

However, there is not enough information to establish an accurate time frame, nor is the death or birth of the Savior referenced. The records are incomplete. There is not enough information to establish in which seal Christ was born. We do, however, have the following statement:

> For they would not hearken unto his voice, nor believe on his Only Begotten Son, even him whom he declared should come *in the meridian of time*, who was prepared from before the foundation of the world. (Moses 5:57)

This would indicate that Christ was born at some point during the middle seal or the fourth seal (being in the meridian of time). There is no information that would lead us to believe that Christ was born exactly four thousand years after Adam, or even during the fifth seal. This is also supported when we compare our modern history with the information found in the book of Revelation. It has been established that Herod died in the year 4 BC. Because Herod was alive when Christ was born, it would be safe to say that Christ was born prior to his death in 4 BC. Many Church scholars, including James E. Talmage and Bruce R. McConkie, have noted this.

The book of Revelation refers to many events of the sixth seal that have yet to take place.

> And I beheld when he had opened the sixth seal, and, lo, there was a *great earthquake*; and the *sun became black* as sackcloth of hair, and the *moon became as blood*;
>
> And the *stars of heaven fell* unto the earth, even as a fig tree casteth her untimely figs, when she is shaken of a mighty wind.
>
> And the *heaven departed as a scroll* when it is rolled together; and *every mountain and island were moved out of their places*. (Revelation 6:12–14)

And after these things I saw four angels standing on the four corners of the earth, *holding the four winds of the earth, that the wind should not blow on the earth,* nor on the sea, nor on any tree.

And I saw another angel ascending from the east, having the seal of the living God: and he cried with a loud voice to the four angels, to whom it was given to hurt the earth and the sea,

Saying, *Hurt not the earth,* neither the sea, nor the trees, *till we have sealed the servants of our God in their foreheads.*

And I heard the number of them which were sealed: and *there were sealed an hundred and forty and four thousand of all the tribes of the children of Israel.* (Revelation 7:1–4)

Because these events of the sixth seal—a worldwide earthquake where every mountain and island is moved out of place, the calling of the 144,000, and the winds being released upon the earth—have not come to pass in the last two thousand years, we know that the time of the sixth seal is not completed.

If the days have not been shortened—and at this point we have no reason to believe that they have been—and because there have been more than two thousand years between the birth of Christ and the present day, we can also safely conclude, for the purposes of our discussion, that Christ was indeed born in the fourth seal, in the meridian of time.

As we try to piece together the dates and times, it becomes evident that there is a lack of information for a reason. The Lord requires faith, prayer, obedience, searching, and pondering. Just as the magi watched for the signs of Christ's birth, so we are to watch for the signs of His return. In similar fashion, we can search the scriptures to more fully understand the signs and to prepare ourselves temporally and spiritually. The Lord revealed certain information to the Nephites on this topic; however, He saw fit to exclude it from the Book of Mormon.

And he *did expound all things, even from the beginning until the time that he should come in his glory*—yea, even all things which should come upon the face of the earth, even until the elements should melt with fervent heat, and the earth should be wrapt together as a scroll, and the heavens and the earth should pass away;

And these things have I written, which are a lesser part of the things which he taught the people; and I have written them to the intent that they may be brought again unto this people, from the Gentiles, according to the words which Jesus hath spoken.

Behold, *I was about to write* them, *all which were engraven* upon the plates of Nephi, *but the Lord forbade it*, saying: *I will try the faith of my people.* (3 Nephi 26:3, 8, 11)

The Half Hour of Silence

The half hour of silence is an approximate period of time, signified by the word *about*, which begins at the opening of the seventh seal and continues until the curtain of heaven is unfolded and the face of the Lord is revealed.

And when he had opened the seventh seal, there was *silence in heaven about the space of half an hour.* (Revelation 8:1)

And there shall *be silence in heaven for the space of half an hour,* and immediately after shall the curtain of heaven be unfolded, as a scroll is unfolded after it is rolled up, and the face of the Lord shall be unveiled. (D&C 88:95)

There are several theories on the reason why there will be silence in heaven. The soundest doctrinal response to this query is that silence in heaven will be due to the ever-increasing wicked conditions upon the earth. The following quote from the prophet Joseph Fielding Smith sheds some light on this topic:

In Section 38 of the Doctrine and Covenants, the Lord says, speaking of our day:

"For all flesh is corrupted before Me; and the powers of darkness prevail upon the earth, among the children of men, in the presence of all the hosts of heaven—

"Which causeth silence to reign, and all eternity is pained, and the angels are waiting the great command to reap down the earth, to gather the tares that they may be burned; and, behold, the enemy is combined." (D&C 38:11–12.)

Again, one more passage that I want to read to you, this from Section 63 of the Doctrine and Covenants. In verses 32 and 33 of this Section, the Lord says:

"I, the Lord, am angry with the wicked; I am holding My Spirit from the inhabitants of the earth.

"I have sworn in my wrath, and decreed wars upon the face of the earth, and the wicked shall slay the wicked, and fear shall come upon every man."

Now the Lord has withdrawn His Spirit from the world. Do not let this thought become confused in your minds. The Spirit He has withdrawn from the world is not the Holy Ghost (for they never had that!), but it is the light of truth, spoken of in our scriptures as the Spirit of Christ, which is given to every man that cometh into the world, as you find recorded in Section 84 of the Doctrine and Covenants.

Now because of the wickedness of the world, that Spirit has been withdrawn, and when the Spirit of the Lord is not striving with men, the spirit of Satan is. Therefore, we may be sure that the time has come spoken of in Section 1 of the Doctrine and Covenants, wherein the Lord says: "For I am no respecter of persons, and will that all men shall know that the day speedily cometh; the hour is not yet, but is nigh at hand, when peace shall be taken from the earth, and the devil shall have power over his own dominion." (Verse 35.)

As the Holy Ghost is not taken from the earth, it would be safe to assume that silence in heaven does not mean lack of communication or revelation. I would also point out that it will take a long time for peace to be taken from the earth. This process that will continue until eventually there will be no peace left on earth. Once the 144,000 have completed their mission and the gospel is no longer proclaimed, then Satan will have all power.

Peace *has* been taken from the earth. The devil *has* power over his own dominion. The Spirit of the Lord *has* been withdrawn. Not because the Lord desires to withdraw that Spirit, but because of the wickedness of mankind, it becomes necessary that this Spirit of the Lord be withdrawn.

I would like to read verses 53 and 54 of Section 63.

"These things are the things that ye must look for; and, speaking after the manner of the Lord, they are now nigh at hand, and in a time to come, even in the day of the coming of the Son of Man.

"And until that hour there will be foolish virgins among the wise; and at that hour cometh an entire separation of the righteous and the wicked; and in that day will I send mine angels to pluck out the wicked and cast them into unquenchable fire."

Those days are here. [Joseph Fielding Smith, *The Signs of the Times: A Series of Discussions* (Salt Lake City: Deseret Book, 1970), 110–12.]

We know that there will be extreme wickedness upon the face of the earth during this time, as the events of the seventh seal take place. Satan and his hosts will be at their worst, influencing the wicked inhabitants of the earth. I am sure there was some silence in heaven prior to the flood because of the wicked condition of earth at that time. In this case, it is evident that the silence in heaven is a descriptive reference to the feeling that is felt by the heavenly hosts witnessing to the wickedness and abominations that are taking place in the world. It should also be noted that silence in heaven could be a general condition; however, in the context of the "half hour of silence in heaven" referred to in Revelation 8, this is specific to an event.

To determine when the half hour of silence will begin, we must examine the events that take place prior to the opening of the seventh seal. When all of the events within the sixth seal have transpired, we can know that the seventh seal is ready to be opened. As to the exact time when the seventh and final seal will be opened, we can only guess.

Both John the Revelator and Joseph Smith are specific in their detail. In Revelation 6, John describes some of the events that are to transpire prior to the opening of the seventh seal. In Doctrine and Covenants 88, Joseph also describes these same events.

The following events are what I would call an event sequence, or a series of events that are interlinked. When these events are described in scripture, the manner of language suggests that they are to be considered part of the same event.

And I beheld when he had opened the sixth seal, and, lo, there was *a great earthquake*; and the *sun became black* as sackcloth of hair, and *the moon became as blood*;

And the *stars of heaven fell* unto the earth, *even as a fig tree* casteth her untimely figs, when she is shaken of a mighty wind. (Revelation 6:12–13)

For not many days hence and the *earth shall tremble and reel to and fro* as a drunken man; and *the sun shall hide his face*, and shall refuse to give light; and *the moon shall be bathed in blood*; and *the stars* shall become exceedingly angry, and *shall cast themselves down as a fig* that falleth from off a fig tree. (D&C 88:87)

Thus far we have:

- A great earthquake will cause the earth to tremble.
- The sun will be darkened.
- The moon will be red.
- The stars will appear to be cast down or shaken.

And *the heaven departed as a scroll* when it is rolled together; *and every mountain and island were moved out of their places*. (Revelation 6:14)

For after your testimony cometh *the testimony of earthquakes, that shall cause groanings in the midst of her, and men shall fall upon the ground and shall not be able to stand. . . .*

And immediately there *shall appear a great sign in heaven*, and all people shall see it together. (D&C 88:89, 93)

And now we add:

- There will be a great sign in the heavens.
- The earthquake will be so great that every island and mountain will be moved out of its place, and people will not be able to stand. This will be a worldwide tectonic shifting.

And the *kings of the earth, and the great men*, and *the rich men*, and *the chief captains*, and *the mighty men*, and *every bondman*, and *every free man, hid themselves* in the dens and in the rocks of the mountains;

> *And said* to the mountains and rocks, Fall on us, and *hide us from* the face of him that sitteth on the throne, and from *the wrath of the Lamb.* (Revelation 6:15–16)

> And all things shall be in commotion; and surely, men's hearts shall fail them; for *fear shall come upon all people.* (D&C 88:91)

Finally, fear shall come upon all people.

As an additional note, there is greater detail in the Doctrine and Covenants than in Revelation of this event. Verse 90 in particular talks of thunder, lightning, and the seas heaving themselves beyond their bounds. Atmospheric disturbances, such as thunder and lightning, have always been associated with earthquakes.

Since there is no historical record of this great earthquake with its heavenly signs—as described by the Lord's anointed since the Prophet Joseph penned this revelation on December 27–28, 1832, and January 3, 1833—we know of a surety that it has not taken place.

Speaking of this exact event, the Savior indicates,

> And in that day shall be heard of wars and rumors of wars, and *the whole earth shall be in commotion*, and *men's hearts shall fail them*, and *they shall say that Christ delayeth his coming until the end of the earth.*
>   *And the love of men shall wax cold, and iniquity shall abound.* (D&C 45:26–27)

There is a reason why people shall say Christ delays His coming. After such a tumultuous event of worldwide proportions, the world will literally think that the great day of the Lord is here. It will be after this that man's faith will dwindle even more, fulfilling the above scripture that states the love of men will wax cold, and iniquity will abound.

This great earthquake will be a defining moment in history. The physical devastation will destroy economies and governments, leaving countries in a lawless state. And when Christ does not come, it will cause those who oppose truth to say God does not exist, that people are not accountable, and that a Supreme Being does not govern them.

As the world recovers in what they believe is a new reality on this planet, wickedness will increase. Man's love will wax cold in these godless conditions and will pave the way for the judgments of God to be poured out upon the wicked during the many years before the Second Coming.

As a further testimony that the half hour of silence is yet to come, John describes additional events that are to transpire prior to the opening of the seventh seal:

> And after these things I saw *four angels* standing on the four corners of the earth, *holding the four winds of the earth*, that *the wind should not blow on the earth*, nor on the sea, nor on any tree.
>
> And I saw another angel ascending from the east, having the seal of the living God: and he cried with a loud voice to the four angels, to whom it was given to hurt the earth and the sea,
>
> Saying, Hurt not the earth, neither the sea, nor the trees, *till we have sealed the servants of our God in their foreheads.*
>
> And I heard the number of them which were sealed: and *there were sealed an hundred and forty and four thousand* of all the tribes of the children of Israel. (Revelation 7:1–4)

The sealing of the 144,000 has yet to take place, and the four winds that will hurt the earth and the sea will be released once they have been sealed. Once these events have transpired, the seventh seal can be opened, and the silence in heaven of about the space of half an hour will begin. During this silence in heaven, the judgments of God will be poured out upon the earth, as described by John in the verses and chapters following Revelation 8:1.

To determine the actual length of time this period of silence represents, it is logical to conclude that it is heaven's time. Joseph's account of this event in Section 88 tells us that immediately following the half hour of silence in heaven, the face of the Lord will be revealed. John's account in Revelation describes many events (including plagues, sieges, atrocities, wars, conflicts, and other marvelous events) that will transpire after the half hour of silence in heaven begins. Also, there is the final forty-two months where

Jerusalem will be under siege. Following these events, the face of the Lord is revealed. Because it would be physically impossible for these events to transpire within the space of half an hour of earth's time, using "heaven's time" fits with the amount of time required.

Using the formula of approximately a thousand years of time on earth to equal one day of the Lord's time (see Abraham 3:4; 2 Peter 3:8), a half an hour of heaven's time, as it is reckoned on earth, would be 20.83 years. This calculation is only approximate. John stated that there was silence in heaven about the space of half an hour. A variation of even 30 seconds in heaven would be 126.7 days on earth. Imagine a variation of a couple of minutes in either direction. This would result in a year or two either earlier or later than the expected time.

The next problem is that we have no way of knowing exactly when the seventh seal will be opened. Therefore, we have no point of reference even to begin a calculation. Finally, the Lord states, in referring to the last days,

> And *except those days should be shortened*, there should none of their flesh be saved; but for the elect's sake, according to the covenant, those days shall be shortened. (Joseph Smith—Matthew 1:20)

This would again indicate some change in the time prior to the Lord's coming. With the days being shortened and not equal to the reckoning of time as revealed to Abraham, the ability to make an accurate calculation of this time period is impossible.

It is evident that we are not privy to the day or the hour that the Lord will come. We must watch and be vigilant. A half hour of silence on heaven's clock would allow sufficient time for the judgments of God, as described in Revelation 8–16, to be fulfilled, after which the Lord will return in glory for His millennial reign.

Time, Times, and Half a Time

The phrase *a time, times, and a half*—mentioned in Revelation and in Daniel's prophecies—refers to a time period representing three and a half years. The interpretation of this phrase is as follows:

"time" equals one year, "times" equals two years, and "a half" equals half a year. The phrase occurs in Revelation 12:14 and Daniel 12:7; similar periods of 42 months and 1,260 days are mentioned by John in Revelation, while Daniel mentions periods of 1,290 days and 1,335 days respectively.

Note that 1,260 days are not the exact equivalent of three and a half years; in modern calendars, that is approximately 1,278 days. Even when counting lunar months, there is no precise correspondence. The calendar used by the Hebrews and Babylonians was a solar-lunar one, in which some years consisted of thirteen months. There were twelve years with twelve months and seven years with thirteen months in a nineteen-year period. The Babylonians knew of this nineteen-year cycle in the time of Daniel. The Hebrews also adopted this system around 605 BC, when Palestine fell under Babylonian rule.

In the book of Revelation, John refers to 1,260 days, while Daniel refers to 1,290 days and 1,335 days. Using appropriate combinations of twelve- and thirteen-month years, the numbers mentioned in Revelation 11:3 and 12:6 and Daniel 12:11–12 can be shown to be equivalent to "time, times, and a half."

In actuality, the number of days in a month—in this solar-lunar calendar—sometimes varied by one day because of the day on which the new moon was seen. For the purposes of showing a correlation between 1,260 days, 1,290 days, 1,335 days, and 42 months, a period of 30 days will be used to represent the standard month. (The majority of the months in this calendaring system were composed of thirty-day periods.)

The first line of the following table shows a year and a half, two and a half years, and half of a year, for a total of 1,260 days. The second line of the table shows a year of thirteen months, two years of twelve months, and half a year of twelve months, for a total of 1,290 days. The third line shows a year of twelve months, two years of thirteen months, and half a year of thirteen months, for a total of 1,335 days. There are, of course, other combinations, besides the ones shown here.

Time (One Year)	Times (Two Years)	Half (Half a Year)	Total (Three and a Half Years)
12 x 30 = 360	2 x 12 x 30 = 720	12 x 30 / 2 = 180	1,260 days
13 x 30 = 390	2 x 12 x 30 = 720	12 x 30 / 2 = 180	1,290 days
12 x 30 = 360	2 x 13 x 30 = 780	13 x 30 / 2 = 195	1,335 days

According to these calculations of the calendar that was used by the Hebrews, the numbers provided by John and Daniel are representative of forty-two months, or the duration of the "time, times, and a half." The following scriptures show all of the references to this specific time period:

Time Reference 1

> And I will give power unto my two witnesses, and they shall prophesy *a thousand two hundred and threescore days*, clothed in sackcloth. (Revelation 11:3)

> And the woman fled into the wilderness, where she had a place prepared of God, that they should feed her there *a thousand two hundred and threescore years*. (Joseph Smith Translation—Revelation 12:6)

It should be noted that in the Joseph Smith Translation of the Bible, it replaces the word *days* with *years*. This is no longer a time reference to the last forty-two-month period.

> And from the time that the daily sacrifice shall be taken away, and the abomination that maketh desolate set up, there shall be *a thousand two hundred and ninety days*.
> Blessed is he that waiteth, and cometh to the *thousand three hundred and five and thirty days*. (Daniel 12:11–12)

Time Reference 2

> And to the woman were given two wings of a great eagle, that she might fly into the wilderness, into her place, where she is nourished for *a time, and times, and half a time*, from the face of the serpent. (Revelation 12:14)

And I heard the man clothed in linen, which was upon the waters of the river, when he held up his right hand and his left hand unto heaven, and sware by him that liveth for ever that it shall be for *a time, times, and an half*; and when he shall have accomplished to scatter the power of the holy people, all these things shall be finished. (Daniel 12:7)

And he shall speak great words against the most High, and shall wear out the saints of the most High, and think to change times and laws: and they shall be given into his hand until *a time and times and the dividing of time*. (Daniel 7:25)

Time Reference 3

But the court which is without the temple leave out, and measure it not; for it is given unto the Gentiles: and the holy city shall they tread under foot *forty and two months*. (Revelation 11:2)

And there was given unto him a mouth speaking great things and blasphemies; and power was given unto him to continue *forty and two months*. (Revelation 13:5)

All of these time references appertain to the final winding-up scene prior to the Second Coming.

Times of Refuge

Many individuals have had visions or dreams about the Saints all having to take refuge. Some of these revelations also include the Church asking the Saints to go to places of safety. This is often referred to as "the calling out." In the perilous times ahead, we will be required to go to places of safety. For example, after the worldwide earthquake in the sixth seal, when every island and every mountain is moved out of its place, there will be political, economic, and physical crises on a global scale. During this, there will most likely be times when people will choose to leave their homes or even communities. As we approach the Second Coming, we may not always get to enjoy the comforts and conveniences that are synonymous with peace and prosperity.

Included in these times of refuge is a specific time when the Saints will be required to flee into the wilderness, as Satan will have all power. This particular time when the Church must flee into the wilderness must not be confused with other times when the Saints may be required to seek places of refuge. This is one of the signs, the Lord has identified, that will happen during a specific time period. This time period, being forty-two months in length, happens immediately prior to the Second Coming.

> And to the woman were given two wings of a great eagle, that she might fly into the wilderness, into her place, where she is nourished for *a time, and times, and half a time*, from the face of the serpent. (Revelation 12:14)

In this case, the description of the time when the woman is to flee into the wilderness, as indicated by John, references the last forty-two months prior to the Lord's return. It seems that all of the scripture references related to "time, times, and half a time" (or 42 months, 1,260 days, and such) are specific to this last time frame.

The purpose of the Church fleeing into the wilderness is for the Saints to be in a group of righteous people where combined faith will allow the Lord to protect His Saints and make them terrible to their enemies.

> And it shall be called the New Jerusalem, a land of peace, *a city of refuge, a place of safety for the saints* of the Most High God;
>
> And the glory *of the Lord shall be there, and the terror of the Lord also shall be there*, insomuch that *the wicked will not come unto it*, and it shall be called Zion.
>
> And it shall come to pass *among the wicked*, that every man that will not take his sword against his neighbor *must needs flee unto Zion for safety*.
>
> And there shall be gathered unto it out of every nation under heaven; and it shall be the only people that shall not be at war one with another.
>
> And it shall be said among the wicked: Let us not go up to battle against Zion, for the inhabitants of Zion are terrible; wherefore we cannot stand.

And *it shall come to pass that the righteous shall be gathered out from among all nations, and shall come to Zion*, singing with songs of everlasting joy. (D&C 45:66–71)

Past, Present, and Future

The Prophet Joseph Smith said that the book of Revelation is one of the plainest books [see *Teachings of the Prophet Joseph Smith*, comp. Joseph Fielding Smith (Salt Lake City: Deseret Book, 1938), 290]. At first glance, this does not seem to be the case. There are tons of time references, symbolism, retellings of events, and so on. To the reader, the task appears daunting. Many scholars have gone to great lengths to analyze and offer various explanations of John's message to the world.

Elder Bruce R. McConkie was once asked the question, "Are we expected to understand the book of Revelation?" He answered with the following:

> Certainly. Why else did the Lord reveal it? The common notion that it deals with beasts and plagues and mysterious symbolisms that cannot be understood is just not true. It is so far overstated that it gives an entirely erroneous feeling about this portion of revealed truth. Most of the book—and it is no problem to count the verses so included—is clear and plain and should be understood by the Lord's people. . . .
>
> He [the Lord] has withheld the sealed portion of the Book of Mormon from us because it is beyond our present ability to comprehend. We have not made that spiritual progression which qualifies us to understand its doctrines. But he has not withheld the book of Revelation, because it is not beyond our capacity to comprehend; if we apply ourselves with full purpose of heart, we can catch the vision of what the ancient Revelator recorded. (Bruce R. McConkie, "Understanding the Book of Revelation," *Ensign*, September 1975)

Sometimes even though most of the book of Revelation is in a relatively plain language, we still require the assistance of the Spirit, as well as study and pondering, to have enlightenment. Nephi tells us that the scriptures are plain to those with the spirit of prophecy (see 2 Nephi 25:4).

Many of the world's scholars have gone to great lengths to offer interpretations of the symbolism found in the book of Revelation. While the Prophet Joseph Smith was a biblical scholar and informed of God, it is more likely that Joseph, when calling the book of Revelation plain, was referring to the underlying message found in Revelation rather than the meanings found in studying the symbolism.

To see the simplicity of the book of Revelation, it is important to understand these events from God's perspective. One must also look past the details to get the storyline and use the details to better understand that storyline. What is the message? Then, once we understand the message, we can examine some of the details and see if there is something more to be learned.

Basically, the book of Revelation highlights certain world events, details the plan of salvation, gives warnings to those who will take heed, and spelling out the consequences of wickedness. In other words, this is what is going to happen, so watch for the signs and obey the commandments or suffer the wrath of a just God as He brings forth judgment according to the laws of eternity.

When analyzing the book of Revelation from a time perspective, it is important to understand that John does not go back in time; rather, he gives past details to help explain future events. John spends many of the latter chapters of Revelation discussing this final period in the earth's pre-millennial history. Occasionally, we see the use of historical details in his description of these future events. Sometimes he retells the same events from a different viewpoint. There is so much going on that it can't be told in a single chapter, or from one point of view. Through the use of additional details and references to other time periods, the reader is enabled to more fully understand the entire event in historical context.

Among the many things that John describes in his revelation is the residence of God.

> And *I saw as it were a sea of glass mingled with fire*: and them that had
> gotten the victory over the beast, and over his image, and over his

mark, and over the number of his name, stand on the sea of glass, having the harps of God. (Revelation 15:2)

It is relevant to note that the planet where God resides is like a sea of burning glass, where all things are manifest before Him—past, present, and future.

The angels do not reside on a planet like this earth;
But they reside in the presence of God, on *a globe like a sea of glass and fire*, where *all things for their glory are manifest, past, present, and future, and are continually before the Lord.* (D&C 130:6–7)

It is clear that John's revelation emanates from the perspective of God. This is the only location from which a vision of the earth's future could come. Is it any wonder that there are historical references as John records details of the earth's passage through mortality, as they are shown him from a globe that projects the past, present, and future? This is part of the great winding-up scene in the history of our world. Heavenly Father, in His revelation to John, wants us to understand the historical significance of these events. For those Saints who will go through this ordeal, God wants them to have the reassurance of His plan for them. As we see and understand God's mercy for His Saints, we will appreciate His love for all mankind and acknowledge the role of agency in the eternal scheme of our existence.

Time, Events, and Seals

In Revelation, John gives event-specific information about each individual seal. These are noteworthy events that either have come to pass or will come to pass in each of the seals. Particular detail is given to the events of the sixth and seventh seals.

The wording in Revelation for the opening of seals two through seven goes as follows: "When he had opened the . . . Seal. . . ." The normal thought process is to expect something to happen immediately or in a timely fashion upon hearing such words. With no obvious way of determining at what point during each seal these events will occur, we must conclude that it is possible that events could happen immediately after the seal is open: fifty years after the seal is open, three hundred years, or (in the case of the latter seals, if the days have been shortened) as many as a thousand or more years. The events that follow the opening of a seal could happen any time in the time frame of that particular seal.

Furthermore, if there are multiple events that are described after the opening of a seal, the times between those events could vary. They could come to pass at the same time, close to the same time, or even centuries apart. For this reason, we cannot assume to know when events will happen—we can simply know that they will happen.

The best way to place events in an area of time is to see if there are other time indicators present. We can look to see if the event is described in another scriptural reference. We can see if the event is part of a larger sequence. We can also see if the event is the outcome of a particular situation, or if the event will cause something to happen. Sometimes the nature of the event is such that certain conditions are required to be present or to have taken place for said event to occur. Those conditions could be economic, political, spiritual, environmental, and so on.

An example of this:

> And the *first* went, and *poured out his vial* upon the earth; and *there fell a noisome and grievous sore upon the men* which had the *mark of the beast, and upon them which worshipped his image*. (Revelation 16:2)

This scripture is in reference to the first of the last seven plagues that are to be poured out of vials upon man. The plague is to be upon those who have the mark of the beast and who worship his image. We have the scriptural information to place this event (the first plague) into a certain area of time.

Revelation 13 describes the rise of Satan's power, its duration, and the conditions that pertain to his dominion over mankind. The rise of the beast has a time reference associated with it.

> And there was given unto him a mouth speaking great things and blasphemies; and *power* was given unto him *to continue forty and two months*. (Revelation 13:5)

As we examine the conditions that will be part of this dominion, we see that the same conditions are also part of the description at the time when the first vial is poured out. As these conditions are part of the reign of the beast, they help us to place the timing of the plagues in those forty-two months.

> *And deceiveth them that dwell on the earth* by the means of those miracles which he had power to do in the sight of the beast; *saying to them* that dwell on the earth, that *they should make an image to the beast*, which had the wound by a sword, and did live.
> And he had power *to give life unto the image of the beast*, that the image of the beast should both speak, and cause that *as many as would not worship the image of the beast should be killed.*
> And *he causeth all*, both small and great, rich and poor, free and bond, *to receive a mark in their right hand, or in their foreheads*. (Revelation 13:14–16)

The last seven plagues start with the first being poured out upon those who have the mark of the beast and who worship his image. The image of the beast and the widespread worship of the mark of the beast is associated with this last forty-two-month period. Once this information is considered, we can know the time period when the last seven plagues will be poured out upon the earth. We know that these plagues are poured out prior to the millennial reign of Christ. We also know that the first plague begins after the forty-two-month reign of the beast begins. Therefore, these plagues happen between the time when Satan has been given all power and the millennial reign of the Lord.

There are also time references for the plagues that are announced with the sounding of a trumpet. After the fourth angel sounds, a message will be sent to the inhabitants of the earth:

> And I beheld, and heard an angel flying through the midst of heaven, saying with a loud voice, Woe, woe, woe, to the inhabiters of the earth by reason of the other voices of the trumpet of the three angels, which are yet to sound! (Revelation 8:13)

The several references to *woe* are important as they help us to establish a time or an approximate sense of when these events are to take place.

The second woe is past; and, behold, the third woe cometh quickly. (Revelation 11:14)

This announcement will take place after the two prophets in Jerusalem are resurrected (see Revelation 11:11). At this point in the timeline, there is only one trumpet left to sound. From time indicators, we can determine that the plagues announced by the trumpets will be happening in the same time period as the plagues being poured out of the vials and the plagues sent by God's prophets as they protect the city of Jerusalem and its inhabitants.

Using parameters and established truths to set the stage, we can incorporate time indicators and references to gain a greater understanding of how God's work will unfold in these latter days.

Understanding time parameters allows us to have a new perspective on the messages in the scriptures. We can more accurately chart the course of events. How and why events are going to happen becomes clear. As our understanding of God's plan increases, so does our confidence in how we must direct our lives. In a similar manner, if we analyze individual events using time and sequence, we gain additional insight and a new perspective.

Summary Points

- The time measurement for the length of any one of the seven seals is one day on Kolob.
- The seventh seal is longer than a thousand earth years.
- The seven seals do not overlap.
- One day on Kolob is not always exactly a thousand earth years.
- We live in the time of the sixth seal.
- The use of time and sequence is necessary for understanding the signs of the times.
- There will be a worldwide earthquake in the sixth seal and another in the seventh seal.

- The Church, as a group, will flee into the wilderness during the last forty-two months before the Second Coming of Christ.

- To understand the book of Revelation in context, we must recognize that God lives on a globe where all things are manifest—past, present, and future—and that John is simply communicating a vision that emanates from this realm. A reference to the past can simply be a reference to the past.

- Because of the incredible amount of information about the last forty-two months prior to the Second Coming, John takes many chapters to relay the information, sometimes retelling the same event from a different point of view, or just filling in details.

- The only way to know when an event will happen is to watch it take place. We can be more prepared for an event to happen by understanding the signs that precede it.

- The half hour of silence begins at the opening of the seventh seal.

- Silence in heaven does not mean a lack of revelation.

- During this time, the light of Christ will not strive with mankind because of wickedness.

- The half hour of silence is time in heaven—not time on earth.

- The half hour of silence is an approximate time frame and can't be calculated.

- The half hour of silence is when the Lord will prepare the earth for His return.

- At some point during the half hour of silence, Satan will have all power to afflict people.

- The half hour of silence directly precedes the Second Coming of Jesus Christ.

- Plagues in the last forty-two months prior to the His coming will either be poured out of vials, announced by trumpets, or caused by the two prophets in Jerusalem smiting the earth.

CHAPTER 2: ANALYZING EVENTS

*T*o **understand the** time and sequence of these events, it is helpful to differentiate between the description of a general condition that will exist in the last days and a specific event that is to take place. General conditions often are a voice of warning and testify to the world that the Second Coming of Jesus Christ is near. Specific events are the manifestation of God's judgments upon the world.

When scriptural accounts of these signs and events are analyzed and compared, they can be recognized as singular events, event sequences, or simply general conditions.

As we go through the process of examining events and conditions from a time perspective, we begin to understand the what and when of certain events and conditions. Many events can be clarified by using common sense or by looking for other time indicators.

To assist us in our search to identify or determine if one scripture is referencing another, we can look for similar wording as an indicator. An example of this:

> For not many days hence and the earth shall tremble and reel to and fro as a drunken man; and the sun shall hide his face, and shall refuse to give light; and the moon shall be bathed in blood; and the stars shall become exceedingly angry, and shall cast themselves down as a fig that falleth from off a fig tree.
>
> And after your testimony cometh wrath and indignation upon the people.
>
> For after your testimony cometh the testimony of earthquakes, that shall cause groanings in the midst of her, and men shall fall upon the ground and shall not be able to stand.
>
> And also cometh the testimony of the voice of thunderings, and the voice of lightnings, and the voice of tempests, and the voice of the waves of the sea heaving themselves beyond their bounds.
>
> And *all things shall be in commotion*; and surely, *men's hearts shall fail them*; for fear shall come upon all people. (D&C 88:87–91)

This scripture is describing the worldwide earthquake in the sixth seal. In Doctrine and Covenants 45, we see similar wording, where the Lord is describing the conditions:

> But they shall be gathered again; but they shall remain until the times of the Gentiles be fulfilled.
>
> And in that day shall be heard of wars and rumors of wars, and *the whole earth shall be in commotion, and men's hearts shall fail them,* and they shall say that Christ delayeth his coming until the end of the earth. (D&C 45:25–26)

By looking at the time information, we can see that Israel has been gathered, and it is nearing when the time of the Gentiles is fulfilled. This information lets us know a general time period. Additional information, such as the wars and rumors of wars, reaffirms this.

We are also told that, when the whole earth shall be in commotion, men's hearts will fail them. Why would people say that Christ delays His coming until the end of the earth? It is because there has been an event of such magnitude that the world would believe Christ should have come—such as the worldwide earthquake, described in Section 88.

In this way, we can put together the pieces of the puzzle in our analysis of the time and sequence of events in the last days.

John also describes this same earthquake with similar wording in the following scripture.

> And the kings of the earth, and the great men, and the rich men, and the chief captains, and the mighty men, and every bondman, and every free man, *hid themselves in the dens and in the rocks of the mountains*;
>
> And said to the mountains and rocks, Fall on us, and *hide us from the face of him that sitteth on the throne, and from the wrath of the Lamb:*
>
> For the great day of his wrath is come; *and who shall be able to stand?* (Revelation 6:15–17)

Revelations recorded by John the Revelator and by Joseph Smith describe fear coming upon mankind because of the great earthquake.

As the Lord establishes His word by the mouths of His witnesses, it is not by chance that we see the same events being described by two or more prophets and referenced more than once.

> In the mouth of two or three witnesses shall every word be established. (2 Corinthians 13:1; D&C 6:28)

Dissimilar Events

When comparing one scripture to another, being able to determine if the events described are the same or are different allows us to better understand the situation and often details surrounding it. To illustrate this point, let us examine some prophecies about earthquakes. The earthquake described in Revelations 6:12–14, where "every mountain and island were moved out of their places" is not the same earthquake as the one in Revelation 16:18–21, where "a great earthquake, such as was not since men were upon the earth, so mighty an earthquake, and so great."

In this case, there are enough differences that we are evidently not talking about the same earthquake.

And I beheld *when he had opened the sixth seal,* and, lo, there was a great earthquake; and the sun became black as sackcloth of hair, and the moon became as blood;

And the stars of heaven fell unto the earth, even as a fig tree casteth her untimely figs, when she is shaken of a mighty wind.

And the heaven departed as a scroll when it is rolled together; and *every mountain and island were moved out of their places.* (Revelation 6:12–14)

And there were voices, and thunders, and lightnings; and there was a great earthquake, such as was not since men were upon the earth, so mighty an earthquake, and so great.

And the great city was divided into three parts, and the cities of the nations fell: and great Babylon came in remembrance before God, to give unto her the cup of the wine of the fierceness of his wrath.

And *every island fled away, and the mountains were not found.*

And there fell upon men *a great hail out of heaven, every stone about the weight of a talent:* and men blasphemed God because of the plague of the hail; for the plague thereof was exceeding great. (Revelation 16:18–21)

Note that in Revelation 8, the seventh seal is opened. This chapter then goes on to describe the events that follow the beginning of the seventh seal.

In Revelation 6, every mountain and island is moved out of its place; in Revelation 16, every island flies away and every mountain is not found. In Revelation 6, there is no hail; in Revelation 16, there is a great hail out of heaven, with every stone being about the weight of a talent. In Revelation 6, the earthquake happens after the opening of the sixth seal. In Revelation 16, the earthquake happens after the opening of the seventh seal.

The events surrounding these earthquakes are described in specific enough detail for us to see that they are separate events and will occur at different times.

The Same Event

Now let us reexamine the earthquake referenced in Revelation 16:18–21, using the earthquake in Revelation: 11:19 as a means of comparison. Here we see that the earthquakes described refer to the same event. Remember that in chapter 8, the seventh seal is opened. The earthquake described in chapters 11 and 16 is part of John's description of the events that follow the opening of the seventh seal. This is an example of John retelling an event from a different perspective in a different chapter. This allows us to see what is going on and to collect additional details to assist us in forming a mental picture of the event.

> And there were *voices*, and *thunders*, and *lightnings*; and there was a *great earthquake*, such as was not since men were upon the earth, so mighty an earthquake, and so great.
>
> And the great city was divided into three parts, and the cities of the nations fell: and great Babylon came in remembrance before God, to give unto her the cup of the wine of the fierceness of his wrath.
>
> And every island fled away, and the mountains were not found.
>
> And there fell upon men a *great hail* out of heaven, every stone about the weight of a talent: and men blasphemed God because of the plague of the hail; for the plague thereof was exceeding great. (Revelation 16:18–21)

> And the temple of God was opened in heaven, and there was seen in his temple the ark of his testament: and there were *lightnings*, and *voices*, and *thunderings*, and an *earthquake*, and *great hail*. (Revelation 11:19)

In these similarities (lightnings, voices, great hail, and so on), there is one slight variation: an earthquake versus a great earthquake. The earthquake described in Revelation 16 has more detail than the description of the earthquake in Revelation 11; however, a lack of detail does not constitute sufficient grounds to reach a conclusion one way or the other.

If we look beyond these immediate details, we find that prior to the earthquake in chapter 11, there appears to be a great winding-up scene with a siege of forty-two months, where the wicked tread down the holy city except for the temple in Jerusalem, where two prophets are pouring out plagues upon the earth.

> But the court which is without the temple leave out, and measure it not; for it is given unto the Gentiles: and the holy city shall they tread under foot forty and two months.
>
> And I will give power unto my two witnesses, and they shall prophesy a thousand two hundred and threescore days, clothed in sackcloth. . . .
>
> And if any man will hurt them, fire proceedeth out of their mouth, and devoureth their enemies: and if any man will hurt them, he must in this manner be killed.
>
> *These have power to shut heaven, that it rain not* in the days of their prophecy: and have *power over waters to turn them to blood, and to smite the earth with all plagues, as often as they will.* (Revelation 11:2–3, 5–6)

To end the siege, there is a great battle. The end of the battle seems to indicate the beginning of the millennial reign:

> And the seventh angel sounded; and there were great voices in heaven, saying, the kingdoms of this world are become the kingdoms of our Lord, and of his Christ; and he shall reign for ever and ever. (Revelation 11:15)

Lightnings, voices, thunderings, an earthquake, and great hail follow this announcement.

Prior to the earthquake in Revelation 16:5, there is a period of forty-two months where power is given to the beast. As described in the first verse of this chapter, plagues are being poured out upon the earth (represented by the seven angels with seven vials).

At the end of this period, the wicked nations are gathered to a great battle in the holy land.

> For they are the spirits of devils, working miracles, which go forth
> unto the kings of the earth and of the whole world, to gather them
> to the battle of that great day of God Almighty. (Revelation 16:14)

At the end of these events, we have an announcement that indicates the end of wickedness.

> And the seventh angel poured out his vial into the air; and there came
> a great voice out of the temple of heaven, from the throne, saying, It
> is done. (Revelation 16:17)

Lightnings, voices, thunderings, a great earthquake, and great hail also follow this announcement.

From the unmistakable similarities surrounding these events, we can conclude with certainty that these two earthquakes are the same event being described in different chapters by John as he unfolds the scenes of the last days. This is significant because John revisits the last terrible period prior to the millennial reign described in Revelation 11 again in chapter 16. By understanding that John described a single event in two separate chapters, we can more accurately place any events of these chapters in a time sequence.

Whenever we have detail in the descriptions of events, it can assist us in understanding time and sequence. Our task is to search, ponder, and pray to understand such details. It would appear that John revisits the events of this period to present additional information. We can now match up these events to get a better understanding of what will happen, as both accounts provide different details from different perspectives.

As we continue to explore chapters in Revelation, we will see other similarities that will add more information and insight as John revisits this last forty-two-month period from yet other perspectives. In addition to the plagues that are poured out of vials, it appears that the plagues announced by trumpets are also associated with this last time period. This connection will be discussed later on. We begin to see how interwoven the chapters of Revelation are, as there are at least three different accounts of the plagues: those announced by trumpets, those poured out of vials, and those that are a result of the two prophets in Jerusalem who smite the earth.

This type of analysis helps us understand the same event. Sometimes the same event is in completely different books, such as Daniel in the Old Testament, Revelation in the New Testament, or the Doctrine and Covenants.

General Conditions

We have examined the descriptions of specific events; now let us turn to some examples of descriptions that are more representative of general conditions that will exist in the last days and the implications that these descriptions have for us. Though some prophecies are specific in nature, others are more general. This is important to understand the context of the prophecy, thereby determining if the prophecy has been fulfilled, is waiting to be fulfilled, or is in the process of being fulfilled.

The prophecies of Joel, John the Revelator, and Joseph Smith all talk of the moon turning to blood, or being bathed in blood, and the sun being turned into darkness, or darkened. Joel states,

> The sun shall be turned into darkness, and the moon into blood, before the great and the terrible day of the Lord come. (Joel 2:31)

In our time, we have seen several blood moons. History has also recorded occasions when the sun has been darkened for extended periods. In this manner, sometimes the scriptures refer to a condition, while other times they refer to a specific event. As we examine blood moons and the darkening of the sun, we will see how they can be part of an event sequence and some of the consequences that can happen as a result.

Blood Moons

In our day, there are, have been, and will continue to be times when the moon appears to be bathed in blood. Some of these are called "blood moons" and occur during solar and lunar eclipses. And at other times, atmospheric conditions cause the moon to appear red. There are several situations that can cause a red moon. The following excerpt is from an article that describes some of the conditions that will cause a red moon:

> The most common way to see the Moon turn red is when the Moon is low in the sky, just after moonrise or before it's about to set below the horizon. Just like the Sun, light from the Moon has to pass through a larger amount of atmosphere when it's down near the horizon, compared to when it's overhead.
>
> The Earth's atmosphere can scatter sunlight, and since moonlight is just scattered sunlight, it can scatter that too. Red light can pass through the atmosphere and not get scattered much, while light at the blue end of the spectrum is more easily scattered. When you see a red moon, you're seeing the red light that wasn't scattered, but the blue and green light have been scattered away. That's why the Moon looks red.
>
> The second reason for a red moon is if there's some kind of particle in the air. A forest fire or volcanic eruption can fill the air with tiny particles that partially obscure light from the Sun and Moon. Once again, these particles tend to scatter blue and green light away, while permitting red light to pass through more easily. When you see a red moon, high up in the sky, it's probably because there's a large amount of dust in the air.
>
> A third—and dramatic—way to get a red moon is during a lunar eclipse. This happens when the Moon is full and passes into Earth's shadow (also known as the umbra), which darkens it. At that point, the Moon is no longer being illuminated by the Sun. However, the red light passing through the Earth's atmosphere does reach the Moon, and is thus reflected off of it.
>
> For those observing from the ground, the change in color will again be most apparent when the Moon appears low in the night sky, just after moonrise or before it's about to set below the horizon. Once again, this is because our heavy atmosphere will scatter away the blue/green light and let the red light go straight through. (Matt Williams, "A Red Moon—Not a Sign of Apocalypse," *Universe Today*, November 1, 2014)

Blood moons occur frequently and are a general condition in our day. However, in spite of the general conditions that exist, there are references to the moon turning to blood that are event specific—the worldwide earthquake that will happen in the sixth seal, for example:

> And I beheld when he had opened the sixth seal, and, lo, there was a great earthquake; and the sun became black as sackcloth of hair, and the moon became as blood;
>
> And the stars of heaven fell unto the earth, even as a fig tree casteth her untimely figs, when she is shaken of a mighty wind.
>
> And the heaven departed as a scroll when it is rolled together; and every mountain and island were moved out of their places.
>
> And the kings of the earth, and the great men, and the rich men, and the chief captains, and the mighty men, and every bondman, and every free man, hid themselves in the dens and in the rocks of the mountains. (Revelation 6:12–15)

In this case, we have a sequence of events, where one thing follows another. A worldwide earthquake would undoubtedly result in some volcanic activity, especially when every mountain and every island is moved out of its place. This, in turn, would cause the moon to become as blood and the sun as black as sackcloth of hair. As a result of this sequence of events, we have a time when the scriptures refer to a blood moon as a specific event and not a general event.

Sun Darkened

The following historical information on volcanic activity gives us an idea of some of the conditions that have already come pass in the last two millennia.

> Stothers found that tree-ring and ice-core data frequently supported the connections he'd made between historical events and volcanoes. Ancient historians described dry fogs, dark skies, poor harvests and heavy snowfall in the year 536. "The sun became dark and its darkness lasted for 18 months," wrote Michael the Syrian. "Each day it shone for about 4 hours, and still this light was only a feeble shadow. Everyone declared that the sun would never recover its full light. The fruits did not ripen and the wine tasted like sour grapes." An examination

of tree rings from the year 536 revealed extremely narrow rings in trees from around the world. The combined evidence, Stothers concludes, points to a volcanic aerosol cloud that persisted more than a year. The cloud spread over the entire northern half of the planet, but because no eruption was observed or recorded at the time, Stothers cannot say exactly where it occurred.

Stothers found signs of another unknown volcano that erupted 90 years later. "In the year A.D. 626," wrote Michael the Syrian, "the light of half the sphere of the sun disappeared, and there was darkness from October to June. As a result people said that the sphere of the sun would never be restored to its original state." Greenland ice-core samples dating from the year 626 are very acidic—so much so that the volcano that led to them may have been one of the greatest producers of volcanic aerosols in recorded history. Furthermore, bristlecone pine trees in California show evidence of a summer frost in 628, which indicates that the massive aerosol cloud produced by the 626 volcano spanned the entire globe for at least two years. Scientists are still looking for evidence that would identify which volcano was responsible; it may have been one in Iceland. (Richard B. Stothers and Michael R. Rampino, "Volcanic eruptions in the Mediterranean before A.D. 630 from written and archaeological sources," *Journal of Geophysical Research*, August 10, 1983)

Darkening skies in 1815–16 has the following explanation:

Evidence suggests the anomaly was caused by a combination of a historic low in solar activity with a volcanic winter event, the latter caused by a succession of major volcanic eruptions capped by the 1815 eruption of Mount Tambora, in the Dutch East Indies (Indonesia), the largest known eruption in over 1,300 years.

The following year, 1816, is known as the Year Without a Summer, also the Poverty Year, the Summer that Never Was and the Year There Was No Summer

Impact: Caused a volcanic winter that dropped temperatures, by 0.4–0.7 °C or 0.7–1.3 °F, worldwide. Eighteen Hundred and Froze to Death, because of severe summer climate abnormalities that caused average global temperatures to decrease by 0.65 degrees. This resulted in major food shortages across the Northern Hemisphere. [Richard B. Stothers, "The Great Tambora Eruption in 1815 and Its Aftermath," *Science* 224 (1984), 1191–1198]

And the following discusses ice core research:

> Ice cores from the Antarctic and Iceland show the volcanic activity of the planet over the last 4,100 years. This activity is more frequent and explosive in the past 2,000 years than in the previous 2,100.
>
> Over all there is an average of 1.3 eruptions per century for a total of 53 eruptions. In the last 1,000 years there have been nine large, low latitude eruptions that contributed significant amounts of volcanic aerosol to the atmosphere of both hemispheres, potentially affecting global climate. In the previous 1,000 years there were only two eruptions of this magnitude. [Jihong Cole-Dai, Ellen Mosley-Thompson, Shawn P. Wight, and Lonnie G. Thompson, "A 4,100-year record of explosive volcanism from an East Antarctica ice core," *Journal of Geophysical Research*, Vol. 105, No. D19 (October 16, 2000), 24, 431–24, 441]

Author's note: After having read several accounts of the year 1816, it becomes quite evident that northern Europe, the northeastern United States, and eastern Canada suffered temperatures averaging between five and ten degrees below normal during June, July, and August, which included frequent frosts and even up to ten inches of snow. It was only the warmer fall and winter that managed to pull up the mean temperatures for the year. These conditions caused starvation, death, and sickness. It is also suspected that these conditions were responsible for the onset of the typhus epidemic that killed millions between 1817 and 1819.

Once we understand that the sun being darkened or the moon becoming as blood can be specific to an event or a general condition, we also understand that the prophecy of Joel is probably a general condition. This was confirmed in October conference of 2001 in a talk entitled "Living in the Fullness of Times," when President Gordon B. Hinckley declared that the prophecy of Joel had been fulfilled. In contrast, we are still waiting for the moon to turn to blood as part of the event sequence that will happen during the great earthquake that is described in Revelation 6.

Rainbow Withdrawn

The Prophet Joseph Smith received a prophecy and a revelation regarding the rainbow:

> I have asked of the Lord concerning His coming; and while asking the Lord, He gave a sign and said, "In the days of Noah I set a bow in the heavens as a sign and token that in any year that the bow should be seen the Lord would not come; but there should be seed time and harvest during that year: but whenever you see the bow withdrawn, it shall be a token that there shall be famine, pestilence, and great distress among the nations, and that the coming of the Messiah is not far distant." (Joseph Smith, *Teachings of the Prophet Joseph Smith*, 340–41)

Our history indicates that the sun has been darkened for periods of up to eighteen months at a time. During this time, it is possible that there were no rainbows in a given year. With the events yet to come in the sixth seal, there may well be periods of a year or more when the sun will again be darkened. This would indicate a time of pestilence, famine, and great distress. It would appear that there might be more than one year that the bow will not be seen. Therefore, we are left to watch for all of the signs to be prepared for the time when the Lord will come.

Elements in Our Solar System

It is possible not everything that is a plague or a judgment has been recorded, nor has the frequency or the number of times that God's wrath will be poured out upon the earth. But the information that we do have gives reason for pause. A closer examination of our solar system and planetary history may shed some light on the possibilities of using heavenly resources that are close at hand and how they might be part of the judgments.

> In the outer regions of our solar system, there are unknown quantities of comets. Some estimates are around a trillion.
>
> Short-period comets originate in the Kuiper belt or its associated scattered disc, which lie beyond the orbit of Neptune. Long-period

comets are thought to originate in the Oort cloud, a spherical cloud of icy bodies extending from outside the Kuiper belt to halfway to the next nearest star. Long-period comets are directed towards the Sun from the Oort cloud by gravitational perturbations caused by passing stars and the galactic tide. . . .

In the outer Solar System, comets remain frozen and inactive and are extremely difficult or impossible to detect from Earth due to their small size. . . . As a comet approaches the inner Solar System, solar radiation causes the volatile materials within the comet to vaporize and stream out of the nucleus, carrying dust away with them.

The streams of dust and gas each form their own distinct tail, pointing in slightly different directions. The tail of dust is left behind in the comet's orbit in such a manner that it often forms a curved tail called the type II or dust tail. At the same time, the ion or type I tail, made of gases, always points directly away from the Sun. ("Comet," *Wikipedia*, last modified March 31, 2016)

Comets are usually made up of ice, rock, other debris, and gases. They tend to follow set orbits but are subject to breaking up, like the comet named Shoemaker Levy 9 that broke into fragments and collided with Jupiter in 1994. The largest fragments were over two kilometers in diameter. In addition to breaking up, comets can also leave fragments in their wake. When these fragments enter our atmosphere, they are called meteor showers. The gases from comets can be toxic, combustible, and carcinogenic, like one of the gases—H_2CO or formaldehyde—detected in the tail of Halley's Comet. It seems possible that the following event recorded in Revelation could be the result of a comet or some other heavenly body.

And the third angel sounded, and there fell a great star from heaven, burning as it were a lamp, and it fell upon the third part of the rivers, and upon the fountains of waters;

And the name of the star is called Wormwood: and the third part of the waters became wormwood; and many men died of the waters, because they were made bitter. (Revelation 8:10–11)

Asteroids are similar in composition and are found in an orbital journey around the sun or around planets, like comets.

There are millions of asteroids, many thought to be the shattered remnants of planetesimals, bodies within the young Sun's solar nebula that never grew large enough to become planets. The large majority of known asteroids orbit in the asteroid belt between the orbits of Mars and Jupiter, or are co-orbital with Jupiter (the Jupiter trojans). However, other orbital families exist with significant populations, including the near-Earth asteroids.

The majority of known asteroids orbit within the asteroid belt between the orbits of Mars and Jupiter, generally in relatively low-eccentricity (i.e. not very elongated) orbits. This belt is now estimated to contain between 1.1 and 1.9 million asteroids larger than 1 km (0.6 mi) in diameter, and millions of smaller ones. . . .

Near-Earth asteroids, or NEAs, are asteroids that have orbits that pass close to that of Earth. Asteroids that actually cross Earth's orbital path are known as *Earth-crossers*. ("Asteroid," *Wikipedia*, last modified March 31, 2016)

A news article in June 25, 2009, discusses near-earth asteroids in more detail:

In 1908, the skies over Siberia lit up in a sudden and massive explosion: an asteroid, 40 m wide, had entered earth's atmosphere and was breaking up in a multi-megaton burst. Although the asteroid itself didn't make it to the ground, the shock wave and massive fireball that resulted destroyed 2,000 sq. km of forest, laying waste to the ground below. The Tunguska Event, as it's called, took place in a remote area, so no human lives were lost. If the blast happened over Toronto, London or Shanghai, it would be another story.

Thousands of asteroids, most of them untracked, swarm around our planet; some are over 10 km wide. "Right now, the most probable amount of warning we'll have for an asteroid impact is zero, because we don't know where most of them are." . . . A new program, called Pan-STARRS, will combine the world's most powerful asteroid-tracking telescope with the largest digital camera ever built. The first of four planned telescopes is set to begin its full scientific mission any day now. "In the past 200 years, we've discovered half a million asteroids," he says. The first telescope alone "should find a comparable number in a single year." (Kate Lunau, "Look Out Below," *Maclean's Magazine*, June 25, 2009)

It is certain that the Lord has lots of life-altering materials to choose from in our solar system, and some are sitting nearby. I am sure that our limited knowledge of the Lord's creations is inconsequential by comparison to the knowledge of the Savior. In addition to these materials, there are other forces that can affect our planet.

The sun, our source of light and heat, can also pose a threat. From time to time, the sun can cause damage to the earth by means of a "coronal mass ejection," or a "solar flare."

> On September 1–2, 1859, the largest recorded geomagnetic storm occurred. Aurorae were seen around the world, most notably over the Caribbean; also noteworthy were those over the Rocky Mountains that were so bright that their glow awoke gold miners, who began preparing breakfast because they thought it was morning. . . .
>
> Telegraph systems all over Europe and North America failed, in some cases even shocking telegraph operators. Telegraph pylons threw sparks and telegraph paper spontaneously caught fire. Some telegraph systems appeared to continue to send and receive messages despite having been disconnected from their power supplies. . . .
>
> The coronal mass ejection of September 1, 1859, overwhelmed Earth's own magnetic field, allowing charged particles to penetrate into Earth's upper atmosphere.
>
> Back in 1859 the invention of the telegraph was only 15 years old and society's electrical framework was truly in its infancy. A 1994 solar storm caused major malfunctions to two communications satellites, disrupting newspaper, network television and nationwide radio service throughout Canada. Other storms have affected systems ranging from cell phone service and TV signals to GPS systems and electrical power grids. In March 1989, a solar storm much less intense than the perfect space storm of 1859 caused the Hydro-Quebec (Canada) power grid to go down for over nine hours, and the resulting damages and loss in revenue were estimated to be in the hundreds of millions of dollars. ("Solar Superstorm," *Science News*, October 23, 2003).

When we think of a burning asteroid or a burning ball of plasma from the sun being cast into the ocean, these verses from Revelation 8 come to mind.

And the second angel sounded, and as it were a great mountain burning with fire was cast into the sea: and the third part of the sea became blood;

And the third part of the creatures which were in the sea, and had life, died; and the third part of the ships were destroyed. (Revelation 8:8–9)

Even if we discuss the Lord's ability to work with the elements that exist on the earth, the possibilities are endless. He has the ability to command the elements. From the scriptures, we know that He changed water to wine, fed a multitude from a few loaves, walked on water, calmed the seas, raised the dead, healed the maimed, caused the ground to shake, and lifted the city of Enoch into paradise. Indeed, as the Creator, He has all power in heaven and on earth.

It is when we understand more fully the magnificence and power of God's creations that we gain perspective of the eternal nature of His work and the manner by which He accomplishes His purposes.

Other Terrestrial Events

These heavenly judgments of the seventh seal are not just your average mudslide or tornado—they are events of global consequence. The earth has had a few occasions when events of this nature have happened. Some that come to mind are the earth being divided in the days of Peleg, the great Flood, and the destruction that occurred after the death of the Savior. Third Nephi lists fourteen cities that were completely destroyed at His death. The Book of Mormon indicates that many other great destructions also transpired at that time, for which no details have been given.

In more recent history, we have records of natural disasters. China recorded 830,000 deaths from an 8.0 earthquake in 1556, and Haiti recorded 316,000 deaths from a 7.0 earthquake in 2010. These disasters are probably not as widespread as those recorded in the Book of Mormon at the time of the Savior's death; however, the worldwide earthquake, where every island and every mountain is moved out of its place (which is yet to come in the sixth seal) will make these modern disasters appear inconsequential by comparison. Because we have never had a global catastrophe like a worldwide earthquake in our lifetime, it would be difficult to envision the entire world as ground zero. With interruptions in power, water, transportation, heat, food deliveries, medical assistance, law enforcement, and so on for an extended period of time, the planet would be limping along with little or no national, military, or foreign aid to count on.

In this regard, we are blessed in this day to have the resources to respond to local or regional catastrophes, but this will not always be the case. As wickedness continues on earth, the arm of justice is moving in response; the world is ripening for destruction. In our sheltered circumstances, we do not always consider or realize the awesome power of the Lord or the arsenal of earthly and heavenly materials that are at His command. To help us get a picture of the cosmos and its ability to impact our world, let us examine our planet, solar system, and galaxy in relation to the events of Revelation.

> Our sun, carrying the earth, moon and all the solar system with it, is hurtling through space at a terrific rate of speed. The sun's orbital speed about the hub of the galaxy is 135 miles per second or 504,000 miles per hour (over one half million miles an hour). The solar system is continuously pulled toward the center of the galaxy by gravity, and continually pulled away from the center by centrifugal force. These forces equalize themselves, thus locking the sun into an elliptical orbit about the galaxy's core. But we feel no movement. This traveling continues all day, all night, century after century. There is no evidence that the sun's movement about the galaxy has ever increased its speed or slackened its pace. The system does not run down or lose power or momentum. There is no indication that there is danger of our sun colliding with any of the other 150 billion stars which belong to this system and which also revolve about the galactic core. All this motion is in addition to the 65,500 miles per hour our earth circles about the sun. What supreme order and apparently effortless, perpetual motion. [Lynn M. Hilton, *The Kolob Theorem: A Mormon's View of God's Starry Universe* (Granite Publishing and Distribution, May 2006), 41]

Even a slight shift in galactic alignment or planetary alignment could result in significant movement of the earth's tectonic plates;

hence, with a command, the Lord can bring about an earthquake of worldwide proportions.

The analysis of events and conditions gives us a greater appreciation for the fact that these events are under the control of the Creator. It also helps us realize the degree to which the wickedness of people plays a role in how the eternal law of justice operates in conjunction with the calamities that we face. The increasing calamities in our day testify so strongly of the need for mankind to repent.

We live in a world with two conflicting messages. The adversary wants us to be lulled into carnal security with the message that all is well in Zion, and the Lord is trying to wake us up to the reality of the plight that we are in. As we continue to examine the calamities that await, we will see this message from God in the in the writings of the prophets. One of the more devastating plagues that awaits us will be the abomination of desolation.

Summary Points

- The increasing calamities are a message from God.
- When the rainbow is withdrawn, it is a sign that there will be famine and pestilence.
- The Lord will return in a year when there is no rainbow.
- Volcanic eruptions could be the cause of feeble sunlight and crop failure.

CHAPTER 3: THE ABOMINATION OF DESOLATION

*T*he *abomination of* desolation, similar to the moon being bathed in blood, is another example of a condition spoken of in general terms and also an event spoken of in specific terms. The prophet Daniel spoke prophetically of a day when there would be "the abomination that maketh desolate" (Daniel 11:31; 12:11). In the New Testament, we also read of "the abomination of desolation, spoken of by Daniel the prophet" (Matthew 24:15).

Speaking about the specific nature of this event, the Bible Dictionary states,

> Conditions of desolation, born of abomination and wickedness, were to occur twice in fulfillment of Daniel's words. The first was to be when the Roman legions under Titus, in A.D. 70, laid siege to Jerusalem. (Bible Dictionary, "Abomination of Desolation"; see also Joseph Smith—Matthew 24:1–2; D&C 45:16, 20)

Jesus speaks of this when telling His disciples of the events of the last days:

> And again shall the abomination of desolation, spoken of by Daniel the prophet, be fulfilled. (Joseph Smith—Matthew 24:32)

John also speaks of this event:

> And the holy city shall they tread under foot forty and two months. (Revelation 11:2)

During this time, the only defense for the inhabitants of the city will be the two prophets of the Lord, keeping the forces of evil at bay. As we read in Revelation about the wicked conditions surrounding this period of time and the oppression of the Jews, it is evident that this is the event Jesus was describing to His disciples:

> For then, in those days, shall be great tribulation on the Jews, and upon the inhabitants of Jerusalem, such as was not before sent upon Israel, of God, since the beginning of their kingdom until this time; no, nor ever shall be sent again upon Israel. (Joseph Smith—Matthew 24:18)

General Terms

In a general sense, the term *abomination of desolation* also describes the judgments of God to be poured out upon the wicked for sinful practices.

> Therefore, tarry ye, and labor diligently, that you may be perfected in your ministry to go forth among the Gentiles for the last time, as many as the mouth of the Lord shall name, to bind up the law and seal up the testimony, and to prepare the saints for the hour of judgment which is to come;
>
> That their souls may escape the wrath of God, the desolation of abomination which awaits the wicked, both in this world and in the world to come. Verily, I say unto you, let those who are not the first elders continue in the vineyard until the mouth of the Lord shall call them, for their time is not yet come; their garments are not clean from the blood of this generation. (D&C 88:84–85)

Phrasing like "the desolation of abomination which awaits the wicked, both in this world and in the world to come" indicates that the abomination of desolation is a consequence or a condition that will be experienced by the wicked.

Nevertheless, let the bishop go unto the city of New York, also to the city of Albany, and also to the city of Boston, and warn the people of those cities with the sound of the gospel, with a loud voice, of the desolation and utter abolishment which await them if they do reject these things.

For if they do reject these things the hour of their judgment is nigh, and their house shall be left unto them desolate. . . .

And verily I say unto you, the rest of my servants, go ye forth as your circumstances shall permit, in your several callings, unto the great and notable cities and villages, reproving the world in righteousness of all their unrighteous and ungodly deeds, setting forth clearly and understandingly the desolation of abomination in the last days. (D&C 84:114–15, 117)

In examining these declarations, the Lord is indicating that the abomination of desolation is a response to, or a consequence of, wickedness. Whether in this life or the next, their houses shall be left unto them desolate.

Blessings cannot come from unrighteousness or ungodly deeds; you cannot reap where you do not sow. The consequence of wickedness is the bleak existence of desolation—pain, suffering, loneliness, and utter emptiness.

The Bible Dictionary gives the following definition for the word *abomination*:

Abomination: An object that excites loathing (Proverbs 12:22); hence an idol (2 Kings 23:13; Isaiah 44:19). The word is also used to denote any heathen or immoral practice (Deuteronomy 18:9, 12; 20:18); also the flesh of prohibited animals (Leviticus 11:10–13), etc.

The abomination part of the term *abomination of desolation* can be summed up as being the acts of mankind that that are abominable in the sight of the Lord. The consequences of the sword of justice upon these unholy acts often results in conditions of desolation that are numerous and unpleasant. As we read about all of the judgments of God that will be poured out upon the earth, they all fall, in general terms, under the word *desolation*. The abomination of desolation, in general, encompasses the judgments of God in consequence of people's abominable acts. What is certain is that as wickedness increases in the earth, so will the judgments of God in proportion.

A Specific Event

The abomination of desolation, as a specific event, is to take place in the last days. To understand more fully the type of desolation to which the Lord is referring in the last days, we need only examine the footnote for the word *scourge* in the following passage of scripture.

> And there shall be men standing in that generation, that shall not pass until they shall see an overflowing scourge; for a desolating sickness shall cover the land.
>
> But my disciples shall stand in holy places, and shall not be moved; but among the wicked, men shall lift up their voices and curse God and die. (D&C 45:31–32)

The footnote for the word *scourge* refers us to Doctrine and Covenants 29:

> But, behold, I say unto you that before this great day shall come the sun shall be darkened, and the moon shall be turned into blood, and the stars shall fall from heaven, and there shall be greater signs in heaven above and in the earth beneath;
>
> And there shall be weeping and wailing among the hosts of men;
>
> And there shall be a great hailstorm sent forth to destroy the crops of the earth.
>
> And it shall come to pass, because of the wickedness of the world, that I will take vengeance upon the wicked, for they will not repent; for the cup of mine indignation is full; for behold, my blood shall not cleanse them if they hear me not.
>
> Wherefore, I the Lord God will send forth flies upon the face of the earth, which shall take hold of the inhabitants thereof, and shall eat their flesh, and shall cause maggots to come in upon them;
>
> And their tongues shall be stayed that they shall not utter against me; and their flesh shall fall from off their bones, and their eyes from their sockets;

And it shall come to pass that *the beasts of the forest and the fowls of the air shall devour them up.*

And the great and abominable church, which is the whore of all the earth, *shall be cast down by devouring fire*, according as it is spoken by the mouth of Ezekiel the prophet, who spoke of these things, which have not come to pass but surely must, as I live, for *abominations shall not reign.* (D&C 29:14–21)

The timing of this event seems similar to John's description of the aftermath of the abomination mentioned in Revelation. Both events take place at the same time as the destruction of Babylon.

And I saw an angel standing in the sun; and he cried with a loud voice, *saying to all the fowls* that fly in the midst of heaven, Come and *gather yourselves together unto the supper of the great God*;

That ye may eat the flesh of kings, and the flesh of captains, and the flesh of mighty men, and the flesh of horses, and of them that sit on them, and *the flesh of all men*, both free and bond, both small and great.

And I saw the beast, and the kings of the earth, and their armies, gathered together to make war against him that sat on the horse, and against his army.

And the beast was taken, and with him the false prophet that wrought miracles before him, with which he deceived them that had received the mark of the beast, and them that worshipped his image. These *both were cast alive into a lake of fire burning with brimstone.*

And *the remnant were slain* with the sword of him that sat upon the horse, which sword proceeded out of his mouth: and *all the fowls were filled with their flesh.* (Revelation 19:17–21)

A Consequence

In describing how the abomination of desolation would come upon us, the Lord states,

Behold, vengeance *cometh speedily upon the inhabitants of the earth*, a day of wrath, a day of burning, a day of desolation, of weeping, of mourning, and of lamentation; and *as a whirlwind it shall come upon all the face of the earth*, saith the Lord.

> And upon my *house shall it begin, and from my house shall it go forth*, saith the Lord;
>
> *First among those among you*, saith the Lord, *who have professed to know my name* and have not known me, and *have blasphemed against me in the midst of my house*, saith the Lord. (D&C 112:24–26)

As a whirlwind, this desolation shall come upon the whole earth. We will see general conditions of desolation that are the result of wickedness; however, the abomination of desolation as a specific event will occur after the daily sacrifice is taken away:

> And *from the time that the daily sacrifice shall be taken away, and the abomination that maketh desolate set up*, there shall be *a thousand two hundred and ninety days*. (Daniel 12:11)

The time reference of 1,290 days links us to that final period before the Savior returns. The meaning of the daily sacrifice is best described in the Joseph Smith Translation of the Bible:

> And not as those high priests who *offered up sacrifice daily*, first *for their own sins*, and *then for the sins of the people*; for *he needeth not offer sacrifice for his own sins, for he knew no sins*; but *for the sins of the people*. And *this he did once, when he offered up himself.* (Joseph Smith Translation, Hebrews 7:26)

The daily sacrifice refers to the process of repentance. When the opportunity for the world to repent has been lost by completely rejecting the gospel, there will no longer be active missionary efforts among the people. The Church will have withdrawn itself and fled into the wilderness.

When the earth is fully ripe, it will be time for the desolation to begin and the devil to have all power in his dominion. (Again, referring to the last forty-two months when the beast is given all power.) This desolation will begin with those who have polluted the holy sanctuary. Thus, as a consequence of wickedness, when the opportunity to repent has been rejected, the abomination will come upon the wicked.

And I heard, but I understood not: then said I, O my Lord, what shall be *the end of these things*?

And he said, Go thy way, Daniel: for the words are closed up and sealed till the time of the end.

Many shall be purified, and made white, and tried; but the wicked shall do wickedly: and none of the wicked shall understand; but the wise shall understand.

And from the time that the daily sacrifice shall be taken away, and the abomination that maketh desolate set up, there *shall be a thousand two hundred and ninety days*. (Daniel 12:8–11)

In verse 8, Daniel asked, "What shall be the end of these things?" The Lord's response was, "A thousand two hundred and ninety days." As we already know, the period of time that Jerusalem will be under siege prior to the coming of the Lord is described in similar terms: "a thousand two hundred and threescore days" (Revelation 12:6). The Lord is warning us to let us know how long we should expect to endure the desolation of abomination when it comes. The Lord also says,

Blessed is he that waiteth, and cometh to the thousand three hundred and five and thirty days. (Daniel 12:12)

Whether this is meant as a warning of how long we must remain vigilant or as a warning and admonition to keep our covenants, we will be blessed for doing so. The reason for the additional time of forty-five days is also likely a reference to Isaiah's prophecy of the "scornful men."

Wherefore hear the word of the Lord, *ye scornful men, that rule this people* which is in Jerusalem. [This is in reference to those in the highest positions who are in control of the world economy and the fate of nations.]

Because ye have said, We have made *a covenant with death*, and *with hell are we at agreement; when the overflowing scourge shall pass through, it shall not come unto us: for we have made lies our refuge, and under falsehood have we hid ourselves* [they think to escape the judgments of God]:

> Therefore thus saith the Lord God, Behold, *I lay in Zion for a foundation* a stone, a tried stone, a precious corner stone, *a sure foundation: he that believeth shall not make haste.* [Here, the Lord indicates that in Zion the believer shall not have to avoid the plague ("make haste"). The sure foundation shall prove a better refuge than lies and covenants with hell.]
>
> Judgment also will I lay to the line, and righteousness to the plummet: and the *hail shall sweep away* the refuge of lies, and the *waters shall overflow* the hiding place. (Isaiah 28:14–17)

At the end of this forty-two-month period, there will be a great earthquake and great hail. In fact, the hailstones are described as weighing a talent. A common heavy talent in New Testament times weighed 130 pounds. The light talent was half that. This measurement used by the Jews was revised from a measurement that originated in Babylon. The Babylonian light talent weighed sixty-seven pounds, and the Roman light talent weighed seventy-one pounds. A hailstorm of this nature would surely be able to break open a hiding place underground.

> And there fell upon men a *great hail* out of heaven, *every stone about the weight of a talent:* and men blasphemed God because of the plague of the hail; for the plague thereof was exceeding great. (Revelation 16:21)

Shortly thereafter, the waters will be commanded to go into the north at the coming of the Lord.

> He shall command *the great deep,* and it *shall be driven back into the north* countries, and the islands shall become one land. (D&C 133:23)

Once the hiding places have been broken open and water has forced the occupants to come out, they would be exposed to the scourge that they had thought to avoid:

> And your covenant with death shall be disannulled, and your agreement with hell shall not stand; *when the overflowing scourge shall pass through, then ye shall be trodden down by it.* (Isaiah 28:18)

Maybe the reason that it will be a blessing for those who wait until 1,235 days have passed is to allow for extra time until the scourge dissipates or passes through.

We will also see the return of the lost tribes. As they return, the scriptures prophesy that to some their return will be terrible indeed.

> Their enemies shall become a prey unto them. (D&C 133:28)

Between the hail that shall break down their refuges, the waters that will flood them out, the scourge that shall take hold of them, and the lost tribes who shall smite them to the earth, it does not appear good for those scornful men who rule the people in Jerusalem.

In any event, the abomination of desolation will be set up in response to general wickedness—and also the wickedness of the Saints. The Book of Mormon, a book for our time, shows us plainly that there exists cycles of righteousness. We also know that the kingdom of God on earth will continue to roll forth until it has filled the earth; this should strengthen our resolve to be vigilant, so we and our posterity will not be among the wicked.

A Voice of Warning

There is a certain underlying principle that must be understood to lend clarity to the magnitude of the warning:

> Wherefore, verily I say unto you that all things unto me are spiritual, and not at any time have I given unto you a law which was temporal; neither any man, nor the children of men; neither Adam, your father, whom I created.
>
> Behold, I gave unto him that he should be an agent unto himself; and I gave unto him commandment, but no temporal commandment gave I unto him, for my commandments are spiritual; they are not natural nor temporal, neither carnal nor sensual. (D&C 29:34–35)

The principle the Lord is trying to teach is when we are instructed (by way of commandment) to do something, it is spiritual. A commandment to build a fire is spiritual. A commandment to build a temple is spiritual. A commandment to have food storage is spiritual. A commandment to grow a garden is spiritual. Why are we commanded to pray over our crops? It is spiritual.

The reason all commandments are spiritual is that obedience is a spiritual process. What we do may be physical, but the process of obedience helps us to be humble and submissive, allowing the Spirit into our lives through righteous living. The Lord can then bless us for our efforts.

The Lord warns us, by way of revelation given to the Prophet Joseph, to prepare to escape the abomination of desolation:

> And I give unto you a commandment that you shall teach one another the doctrine of the kingdom.
>
> Teach ye diligently and my grace shall attend you, that you may be instructed more perfectly in theory, in principle, in doctrine, in the law of the gospel, *in all things that pertain unto the kingdom of God, that are expedient for you to understand;*
>
> *Of things both in heaven and in the earth, and under the earth; things which have been, things which are, things which must shortly come to pass; things which are at home, things which are abroad; the wars and the perplexities of the nations, and the judgments which are on the land; and a knowledge also of countries and of kingdoms.* (D&C 88:77–79)

In the October 2009 general conference, this counsel was again reiterated:

> For members of the Church, education is not merely a good idea— it's a commandment. We are to learn "of things both in heaven and in the earth, and under the earth; things which have been, things which are, things which must shortly come to pass; things which are at home, things which are abroad." (Dieter F. Uchtdorf, "Two Principles for Any Economy," *Ensign*, November 2009)

Do we consider that, to the Lord, "the perplexities of the nations" or "things which must shortly come to pass" pertain to the kingdom of God (D&C 88:79)? Remember that this admonition is by way of commandment. We are admonished to teach these things diligently, while seeking for His grace to attend us. It is the will of God that we study these things prayerfully. As we do this, we will be more prepared, being in the world but not of it. The Lord would have us use this information in the building of the kingdom.

God does not leave us without a reason to prepare this way, for He states,

> *That ye may be prepared in all things* when I shall send you again to magnify the calling whereunto I have called you, and the mission with which I have commissioned you.
>
> Behold, I sent you out *to testify and warn the people*, and it becometh every man who hath been warned to warn his neighbor.
>
> Therefore, they are left without excuse, and their sins are upon their own heads.
>
> He that seeketh me early shall find me, and shall not be forsaken.
>
> *Therefore, tarry ye, and labor diligently, that you may be perfected in your ministry to go forth among the Gentiles for the last time, as many as the mouth of the Lord shall name, to bind up the law and seal up the testimony*, and to *prepare the saints for the hour of judgment which is to come.*

Here, we see that the mission of preparation is twofold: first to proclaim the gospel (seeking out those who will hear His voice) and second to prepare the Saints for the hour of judgment that is to come. We need to hasten the work of preaching and gathering. And we must prepare in other ways so we will be ready for the coming judgments upon the land. We know that in the sixth seal there will be a worldwide earthquake. Please read carefully the chapters on being physically and spiritually prepared.

> That their *souls may escape the wrath of God, the desolation of abomination which awaits the wicked, both in this world and in the world to come.* Verily, I say unto you, let those who are not the first elders continue in the vineyard until the mouth of the Lord shall call them, for their time is not yet come; their garments are not clean from the blood of this generation.

Here is the reason for our study. Through preparation, we can become instruments in the hands of the Lord in accomplishing His work. We will be able to carefully navigate the perilous times, being informed by our learning, and directed by His Spirit in accomplishing His work: helping our brothers and our sisters, that their souls might escape the desolation of abomination.

> *Abide ye in the liberty* wherewith ye are made free; *entangle not yourselves in sin*, but let your hands be clean, until the Lord comes. (D&C 88:80–86)

The Lord has instructed us to maintain our liberty and to do it in a way that will keep us free from sin. There are still fights for liberty that must be won prior to the time when Satan will have all power. We know that the Constitution, which was inspired of God, is being threatened. We also know that therein we have an obligation to defend it. Let our actions be honorable as we seek to maintain liberty.

Time Parameters and Indicators

As we examine the abomination of desolation (in general terms, meaning the judgments of God upon the wicked, or in specific terms, meaning the forty-two-month siege of Jerusalem and the scourge of the earth at that time), it is evident that these time frames will overlap. All of the time references to the abomination as a specific event refer to the final forty-two months (give or take seventy-five days) just prior to the Second Coming.

In the Doctrine and Covenants, the Lord shows it unto us, as He showed it unto His disciples:

> And I will *show it plainly as I showed it unto my disciples* as I stood before them in the flesh, and spake unto them, saying: As ye have asked of me concerning the signs of my coming, in the day when I shall come in my glory in the clouds of heaven, to fulfil the promises that I have made unto your fathers. . . .
>
> But, verily I say unto you, *that desolation shall come upon this generation* as a thief in the night, and *this people shall be destroyed and scattered among all nations.*
>
> And *this temple* which ye now see *shall be thrown down* that there shall not be left one stone upon another.

> And it shall come to pass, that *this generation of Jews shall not pass away until every desolation* which I have told you concerning them *shall come to pass.* (D&C 45:16, 19–21)

This passage of scripture is in reference to the first abomination of desolation, around AD 70.

> And this I have told you concerning Jerusalem; and when that day shall come, *shall a remnant be scattered among all nations;*
> But *they shall be gathered again;* but they shall remain until the times of the Gentiles be fulfilled.

This scripture is speaking more particularly about the tribe of Judah. However, we are seeing in our day people from all of the tribes of Israel continue to gather around the globe, including many from this tribe. This gathering will continue, until at one point the Lord will seal the twelve thousand high priests from the twelve tribes to fulfill the calling of the 144,000.

> And in that day shall be heard of wars and rumors of wars, and *the whole earth shall be in commotion, and men's hearts shall fail them,* and they shall say that Christ delayeth his coming until the end of the earth. (D&C 45:24–26)

This is a reference to the great earthquake during the sixth seal (Revelation 6:12–17; D&C 88:87–93). This disastrous earthquake of global proportions will cause the people of the world will believe that Christ is coming—that the great and terrible day of the Lord is here. When the Lord does not come, they will say that He delays His return.

> And the *love of men shall wax cold, and iniquity shall abound.*
> And when the times of the Gentiles is come in, *a light shall break forth among them that sit in darkness, and it shall be the fulness of my gospel.*

These are the conditions that will occur during the time of the Gentiles. As wickedness increases, the love of mankind will continue to wax cold. The gospel in its fulness will keep rolling forth.

> But *they receive it not*; for they *perceive not the light*, and they turn
> their hearts from me because of the precepts of men.

This is speaking of the gospel being rejected by the world. When
those last missionaries, presumably the 144,000, are called back, we
will know that this is one of the time indicators of when the abomination of desolation will be set up. These two events are interlinked,
as when the last workers leave the vineyard there is a total rejection
of the gospel and thus no more opportunity for the world's inhabitants to partake of the blessings of the Atonement. The Lord will
separate the fruit and cause the vineyard to be burned.

> And *in that generation* shall the *times of the Gentiles be fulfilled*.
>   And there shall be men standing *in that generation*, that shall not
> pass until they *shall see an overflowing scourge*; for *a desolating sickness*
> shall cover the land. (D&C 45:27–32)

This is the final forty-two-month period prior to the Second
Coming. The time of the Gentiles is the period that precedes the
Millennium.

Some indicators for the abomination of desolation as a specific
event are as follows:

- Missionaries recalled (144,000): The gospel has been preached
  for the last time before all power is given to the adversary.
- Time of the Gentiles fulfilled: This refers to the fact that the
  Gentiles have rejected the gospel completely, or that there is so
  much wickedness that the Lord has seen fit to stop missionary
  efforts, as the judgments of God are to be heaped upon the
  people.
- Daily sacrifice taken away: The peoples of the earth have rejected the blessing of the daily sacrifice, or the Atonement.
  Wickedness reigns, and the holy sanctuary has become polluted. God will not be mocked. In His house it shall begin,
  and from there it shall go forth.

The abomination of desolation is just one of the conditions that
will exist in the last forty-two months prior to the Second Coming.

The world will also have to deal with the two prophets in Jerusalem, who will smite the earth with all manner of plagues. This is a time when preaching the gospel is finished—a time when the judgments of God will come upon the earth.

Summary Points

- The abomination of desolation, as a specific event, will occur again in the last forty-two months prior to the Second Coming.
- The Lord requires us to warn our neighbors, that all may be left without excuse and all may have a chance to repent to escape the desolation of abomination, as a general condition. The time is not far off that the abomination of desolation will be a specific condition.
- Abominations lead to desolations, which serve as a warning from the Lord.
- The abomination of desolation is a consequence of wickedness.
- We must also physically and spiritually prepare against the abomination of desolation.

CHAPTER 4: BEGINNING THE SEVENTH SEAL

The beginning of the seventh seal is when the love of mankind will wax cold and iniquity will abound. It is when the 144,000 will preach the gospel for the last time, and the Saints will prepare for the coming of the Lord. It is when we will see the abomination of desolation, and when all manner of plagues will be poured out upon the earth. It is when the Lord will cause the elements and cosmos to smite the earth, and the forces of evil will rage. It is when the Lord will come in power and glory, and when the ten tribes will return and destroy the last of the wicked hosts remaining. It is when, at last, Satan and his hosts will be bound, and peace will reign.

Revelation 8 is where the description of these events begins. The Lord describes this time as a period when the earth will be prepared for His return.

These are the words of the Lord to Joseph Smith when he inquired about the sounding of the trumpets in Revelation 8:

Q. What are we to understand by the sounding of the trumpets, mentioned in the 8th chapter of Revelation?

A. We are to understand that as God made the world in six days, and on the seventh day he finished his work, and sanctified it, and also formed man out of the dust of the earth, even so, in the beginning of the seventh thousand years will the Lord God sanctify the earth, and complete the salvation of man, and judge all things, and shall redeem all things, except that which he hath not put into his power, when he shall have sealed all things, unto the end of all things; and *the sounding of the trumpets of the seven angels are the preparing and finishing of his work, in the beginning of the seventh thousand years—the preparing of the way before the time of his coming.* (D&C 77:12)

This period of time is also known as the half hour of silence. The following events in the sixth seal will have been completed: a world-wide earthquake that causes every island and every mountain to be moved out of its place. As a result, fear will come upon all men, and the world will believe that the great and terrible day of the Lord has come. When the Lord does not come, they will believe that perhaps He has delayed His coming until the end of the earth. The love of people will wax cold, and the world will begin to completely deny Christ. The 144,000 will have been called to preach the gospel to the earth for one last time. Finally, the four winds, being held by the four angels who are standing on the four corners of the earth, will be released.

The half hour of silence, calculated on heaven's time clock, is approximately 20.83 years (remember, John states "about the space of half an hour"). Because it is not possible to accurately calculate the length of time, we can only watch for the signs and prepare. With the possibility of the days being shortened, it could prove to be even more difficult to calculate.

And except those days should be shortened, there should no flesh be saved: but for the elect's sake those days shall be shortened. (Matthew 24:22; see also Joseph Smith—Matthew 1:20; Mark 13:20)

During this eventful period of time, there will be many plagues, natural disasters, wars, evil deeds, miracles, false prophets, anti-Christs, abominations, desolations, and scourges. After opening of the seventh seal, many judgments will come upon the earth. This is the beginning of the preparations for the Lord to come to the earth. With the love of mankind waxing cold and the continual increase in wickedness, carnal people will exercise their agency in following Satan. Once the earth is fully ripe with iniquity, justice will require the Lord to cleanse the earth. The earth will then go through a change for Him to reside on it. Thus, part of the purpose of this last period of time prior to the Second Coming is to allow agency to take its course for the cleansing of the earth to take place. During this time, the righteous will become more righteous and the wicked increase in wickedness. The calamities that are to come are in consequence of wickedness. Thus, the greatest calamities will occur during the last forty-two months before the coming of Christ, when Satan has all power and the wickedness of mankind is at its greatest.

The beginning of the seventh seal is described in Revelation 8–22. As the opening scenes of this last seal are described, we see the preparations of God in consequence of people's choices. After the world-wide earthquake in the sixth seal, mankind has an opportunity to be charitable, to be humble, and to recognize the hand of God in dispensing justice upon the earth.

In the Doctrine and Covenants, we learn that the love of man will wax cold, the world will choose not to believe in the Second Coming of Christ, and wickedness will increase among the nations. As God prepares to pour out His judgments on the earth, He also prepares His mercies for the righteous.

> And when he had opened the seventh seal, there was silence in heaven about the space of half an hour.
>
> And I saw the seven angels which stood before God; and to them were given seven trumpets.
>
> And another angel came and stood at the altar, having a golden censer; and *there was given unto him much incense, that he should offer it with the prayers of all saints* upon the golden altar which was before the throne.
>
> And the smoke of the incense, which came with the prayers of the saints, ascended up before God out of the angel's hand. (Revelation 8:1–4)

Footnotes to the word *incense* in verse 3 reference Leviticus and Numbers:

> And he shall take a censer full of burning coals of fire from off the altar before the Lord, and his hands full of sweet incense beaten small, and bring it within the veil:
>
> And he shall put the incense upon the fire before the Lord, *that the cloud of the incense may cover the mercy seat* that is upon the testimony, *that he die not.* (Leviticus 16:12–13)

> To be a memorial unto the children of Israel, *that no stranger, which is not of the seed of Aaron, come near to offer incense before the Lord;* that he be not as Korah, and as his company: as the Lord said to him by the hand of Moses. (Numbers 16:40)

In our day, the practice of sacrifice has been done away because the law of Moses has been fulfilled. This would also mean that the practice of burning incense has also been done away. However, it seems to hold some relevance, as the angel in Revelation 8:3 is given much incense and has been requested to offer the incense with the prayers of the Saints. In Leviticus, we learn the purpose of the incense was to cover the mercy seat so that those on whose behalf the offering was made would not die.

It is also important to note that, from Numbers, we learn in Old Testament times the sacrifice or offering was performed by the seed of Aaron, or by priesthood authority. This heaven-sent priesthood offering is a special blessing for the Saints at a time when they require protection from the world and the plagues or justice that is to be meted out upon the wicked.

Armed with this insight, we see that our all-merciful God extends His mercies to the Saints. In general, when judgments come upon the earth, like the rain they usually fall upon the righteous and the wicked equally. In this case, it would seem that the faith of the righteous Saints will combine with God's mercy to provide heavenly protection from some of the terrible judgments that will come upon the earth.

And when the seventh seal opens, the hosts of heaven will grieve because of wickedness, causing silence to reign. Seven angels will be given seven trumpets to announce the finishing of the Lord's preparations to come to the earth, with another angel being given incense to offer with the prayers of the Saints to call upon the mercies of God so they will be spared as much as possible from these calamities—a hallowed priesthood blessing from on high. This offering will happen prior to the plagues being poured out upon mankind, and the devil having all power. It may well be that this offering is preparatory for this last time when the Saints will be required to flee into the wilderness.

Time, Times, and Half a Time

This forty-two-month period in the earth's history will be, for all intents and purposes, the final chapter of the continuation of the war in heaven here on earth, except for the brief period at the end of the Millennium. The city of Jerusalem will be under siege. The beast will have power over all the kingdoms of the earth. Anti-Christs will be performing miracles such as calling down fire from heaven. All mankind will be being forced to bend to the world economy of the beast, under the pain of death.

There will be two prophets in Jerusalem who withstand the enemy and smiting the earth with all manner of plagues. The abomination of desolation and its scourge will be in effect. Satan will rage in the earth, causing havoc and waging war on the Saints of God with his forces, while plagues and judgments are poured out upon them from the holy city of Jerusalem. On the North American continent, the righteous from the nations of the world will gather to the New Jerusalem. Zion and its inhabitants will be terrible. In the rest of the world, people everywhere will be lifting up swords against their neighbors.

During this three-and-a-half-year period, the plagues that will be poured out upon the wicked are referenced as follows:

> And I will give power unto my two witnesses, and they shall prophesy
> a thousand two hundred and threescore days, clothed in sackcloth.

> These are the two olive trees, and the two candlesticks standing
> before the God of the earth.
>
> And if any man will hurt them, fire proceedeth out of their
> mouth, and devoureth their enemies: and if any man will hurt them,
> he must in this manner be killed.
>
> These have power to shut heaven, that it rain not in the days of
> their prophecy: and have power over waters to turn them to blood,
> and to smite the earth with all plagues, as often as they will. (Revela-
> tion 11:3–6)

These verses introduce the fact that God's judgments will be
poured out upon the earth through two prophets. That they will have
the ability or permission from God to do this suggests that they will
act in harmony with the mind and will of the Lord.

In the time of Moses, the destroying angel was sent forth to
administer one of the punishments from God. In Revelation, the
use of angels as administering servants to do God's work is certainly
symbolic of the source of these plagues. Like Moses, it would seem
logical that these two prophets will be God's mouthpiece. In similar
fashion, they will go before the world in the power of the priesthood to smite the earth with plagues.

The scriptures lead us to believe that the earth will be smitten
by some of these more than once:

> To smite the earth with all plagues, as often as they will. (Revelation
> 11:6)

Angels with Trumpets and Vials

In the book of Revelation, there are angels who announce the
judgments of God with trumpets. There are also angels who pour
out vials containing the last plagues of God for mankind. And servants of God are given all power to destroy their enemies, to stop
the rains, to turn the waters to blood, and to smite the earth with
all manner of plagues as often as they will.

It appears that the seven judgments announced by the angels
with trumpets are similar in nature to the judgments that are to be

poured out upon the earth by the angels with the vials. In addition, some of the plagues to be poured out upon the earth by the two prophets are also of a similar nature. To what degree these plagues intermingle is not determined. Perhaps the two prophets in Jerusalem are to pronounce the plagues, being God's mouthpiece, and the angels of God will carry out the administration of these plagues.

As God is preparing to send forth His judgments upon the earth, He first sends a warning to the inhabitants thereof that His judgments are coming.

> And the angel took the censer, and filled it with fire of the altar, and cast it into the earth: and there were voices, and thunderings, and lightnings, and an earthquake. (Revelation 8:5)

A footnote for the word *voices* in the verse 5 refers us to the Doctrine and Covenants:

> And also cometh the testimony of the voice of thunderings, and the voice of lightnings, and the voice of tempests, and the voice of the waves of the sea heaving themselves beyond their bounds. (D&C 88:90)

And the Lord will cause that fire from the "altar" should be cast upon the earth. And there will be voices (perhaps the voices of seas heaving themselves beyond their bounds, the voices of tempests, and other voices of nature's calamities) and lightnings and thunderings and an earthquake warning the people of the earth of the coming judgments to be poured out upon them.

These judgments happen during the time when the world rejects the gospel and Satan has all power.

> And *the first went, and poured out his vial upon the earth*; and there fell a noisome and grievous sore *upon the men which had the mark of the beast, and upon them which worshipped his image.* (Revelation 16:2)

For the most part, the descriptions of the plagues, whether they are announced by a trumpet or poured out of a vial, are similar. However, there are a few differences. It could well be that in John's vision certain aspects of these plagues stood out more as he was seeing all of this from different points of view. His task, of course, is to relay the message that Heavenly Father is sending to His children.

Angels will announce the plagues. John describes angels who announce the plagues with the sounding of a trumpet. He also describes angels who pour the plagues out of vials.

Trumpets

> And the seven angels which had the *seven trumpets* prepared themselves to sound. (Revelation 8:6)

Vials

> And I saw another sign in heaven, great and marvellous, seven angels having the seven last plagues; for in them is filled up the wrath of God. . . .
>
> And one of the four beasts gave unto the seven angels *seven golden vials* full of the wrath of God, who liveth for ever and ever.
>
> And the temple was filled with smoke from the glory of God, and from his power; and no man was able to enter into the temple, till the seven plagues of the seven angels were fulfilled. (Revelation 15:1, 7–8)

We know in the scriptures that trumpets are used to herald messages and that wrath is poured out.

It is interesting, in this day of test tubes, that John's vision would use test tubes or vials to pour out plagues, the very tools used in the conjuring or formation of many of the modern-day plagues that are upon the world.

The First Plague

Trumpets

> The first angel sounded, and there followed hail and fire mingled with blood, and they were cast upon the earth: and the third part of trees was burnt up, and all green grass was burnt up. (Revelation 8:7)

Vials

> And the first went, and poured out his vial upon the earth; and there fell a noisome and grievous sore upon the men which had the mark of the beast, and upon them which worshipped his image. (Revelation 16:2)

Footnotes for the word *fire* in Revelation 8:7 refer us to Exodus. This is an interesting description of a similar event in ancient Egypt:

> And the Lord said unto Moses, Stretch forth thine hand toward heaven, that there may be hail in all the land of Egypt, upon man, and upon beast, and upon every herb of the field, throughout the land of Egypt.
>
> And Moses stretched forth his rod toward heaven: and the Lord sent thunder and hail, and the fire ran along upon the ground; and the Lord rained hail upon the land of Egypt.
>
> So there was *hail, and fire mingled with the hail*, very grievous, such as there was none like it in all the land of Egypt since it became a nation.
>
> And the hail smote throughout all the land of Egypt all that was in the field, both man and beast; and the hail smote every herb of the field, and brake every tree of the field. (Exodus 9:22–25)

The Second Plague

Trumpets

> And the second angel sounded, and as it were a great mountain burning with fire was cast into the sea: and the third part of the sea became blood;
>
> And the third part of the creatures which were in the sea, and had life, died; and the third part of the ships were destroyed. (Revelation 8:8–9)

Vials

> And the second angel poured out his vial upon the sea; and it became as the blood of a dead man: and every living soul died in the sea. (Revelation 16:3)

The Third Plague

Trumpets

And the third angel sounded, and there fell a great star from heaven, burning as it were a lamp, and it fell upon the third part of the rivers, and upon the fountains of waters;

And the name of the star is called Wormwood: and the third part of the waters became wormwood; and many men died of the waters, because they were made bitter. (Revelation 8:10–11)

Vials

And the third angel poured out his vial upon the rivers and fountains of waters; and they became blood. (Revelation 16:4)

The Fourth Plague

Trumpets

And the fourth angel sounded, and the third part of the sun was smitten, and the third part of the moon, and the third part of the stars; so as the third part of them was darkened, and the day shone not for a third part of it, and the night likewise. (Revelation 8:12)

Vials

And the fourth angel poured out his vial upon the sun; and power was given unto him to scorch men with fire.

And men were scorched with great heat, and blasphemed the name of God, which hath power over these plagues: and they repented not to give him glory. (Revelation 16:8)

We know that a day of burning is coming for the wicked, and one of the references to this event is:

And they went up on the breadth of the earth, and compassed the camp of the saints about, and the beloved city: and fire came down from God out of heaven, and devoured them. (Revelation 20:9)

The Fifth Plague

Trumpets

And the fifth angel sounded, and I saw a star fall from heaven unto the earth: and to him was given the key of the bottomless pit.

And he opened the bottomless pit; and there arose a smoke out of the pit, as the smoke of a great furnace; and the sun and the air were darkened by reason of the smoke of the pit.

And there came out of the smoke locusts upon the earth: and unto them was given power, as the scorpions of the earth have power.

And it was commanded them that they should not hurt the grass of the earth, neither any green thing, neither any tree; but only those men which have not the seal of God in their foreheads. (Revelation 9:1–4)

This plague will be hurt those who do not have the seal of God in their foreheads, but not unto death.

And to them it was given that they should not kill them, but that they should be tormented five months: and their torment was as the torment of a scorpion, when he striketh a man.

And in those days shall men seek death, and shall not find it; and shall desire to die, and death shall flee from them.

And the shapes of the locusts were like unto horses prepared unto battle; and on their heads were as it were crowns like gold, and their faces were as the faces of men.

And they had hair as the hair of women, and their teeth were as the teeth of lions.

And they had breastplates, as it were breastplates of iron; and the sound of their wings was as the sound of chariots of many horses running to battle.

And they had tails like unto scorpions, and there were stings in their tails: and their power was to hurt men five months. (Revelation 9:5–10)

Vials

And the fifth angel poured out his vial upon the seat of the beast; and his kingdom was full of darkness; and they gnawed their tongues for pain,

And blasphemed the God of heaven because of their pains and their sores, and repented not of their deeds. (Revelation 16:10–11)

The Sixth Plague

Trumpets

And the sixth angel sounded, and I heard a voice from the four horns of the golden altar which is before God,

Saying to the sixth angel which had the trumpet, Loose the four angels which are bound in the great river Euphrates.

And the four angels were loosed, which were prepared for an hour, and a day, and a month, and a year, for to slay the third part of men.

And the number of the army of the horsemen were two hundred thousand thousand: and I heard the number of them.

And thus I saw the horses in the vision, and them that sat on them, having breastplates of fire, and of jacinth, and brimstone: and the heads of the horses were as the heads of lions; and out of their mouths issued fire and smoke and brimstone.

By these three was the third part of men killed, by the fire, and by the smoke, and by the brimstone, which issued out of their mouths.

For their power is in their mouth, and in their tails: for their tails were like unto serpents, and had heads, and with them they do hurt.

And the rest of the men which were not killed by these plagues yet repented not of the works of their hands, that they should not worship devils, and idols of gold, and silver, and brass, and stone, and of wood: which neither can see, nor hear, nor walk:

Neither repented they of their murders, nor of their sorceries, nor of their fornication, nor of their thefts. (Revelation 9:13–21)

Vials

And the sixth angel poured out his vial upon the great river Euphrates; and the water thereof was dried up, that the way of the kings of the east might be prepared.

And I saw three unclean spirits like frogs come out of the mouth of the dragon, and out of the mouth of the beast, and out of the mouth of the false prophet.

For they are the spirits of devils, working miracles, which go forth unto the kings of the earth and of the whole world, to gather them to the battle of that great day of God Almighty. (Revelation 16:12–14)

These plagues and their consequences are not easily understood. It may be that as the time when they will happen draws nearer, we will be blessed with greater understanding. As John brings us the information about these plagues, he also gives us some pearls of wisdom, or, as I like to call them, warnings.

The Warnings of Revelation

In Revelation 10 and 12, John is passing on information to us in a way that is reminiscent of the way the Savior taught. Through parables, the message is not readily discernible. In this case, John's recounting of the heavenly information that he is receiving is more in the form of an episode or historical event that requires us to *seek* understanding.

Even though chapter 10 is full of imagery and symbolism, it has a definite message. For the purposes of a time sequence evaluation, the main focus is the message that is given by the mighty angel and not by the circumstances that surround his presence. He says "that there should be time no longer." The message he is trying to convey is that it is time for the Lord to come and put an end to Satan's rule.

But in the days of the voice of the seventh angel, when he shall begin to sound, the mystery of God should be finished, as he hath declared to his servants the prophets. (Revelation 10:7)

This event occurs in the next chapter, just after the two prophets in Jerusalem are resurrected:

And the seventh angel sounded; and there were great voices in heaven, saying, The kingdoms of this world are become the kingdoms of our Lord, and of his Christ; and he shall reign for ever and ever. (Revelation 11:15)

This announcement indicates that the events of Adam-ondi-Ahman, when the books are opened and Christ receives the keys to the various dispensations (officially putting an end to Satan's rule), have either been completed or will immediately take place.

According to the scriptures, it appears that the process for an angel to sound—at least this angel—takes days. We are told that it will take days for him to begin to sound, and once he has started, we are not apprised of how long he shall sound. This allows days for the events at Adam-ondi-Ahman to be concluded. The other message in this chapter is that John had not yet finished his assignment. He had to continue to prophesy.

Now let us consider what "the mystery of God should be finished" means. What information or works will be revealed or completed in the days following the resurrection of the two prophets in Jerusalem? When the books are opened, much information that is a mystery will become known. When Christ appears for the second time, in glory, it will become knowledge and no longer a mystery. In the millennial era, the knowledge of the Lord will fill the earth. Because Christ will reign personally upon the earth, knowledge will be available, and there will be no mysteries.

In Revelation 12, we notice that there are references to other time periods. This is one occasion when the Lord provides historical perspective to help us to get the full picture. John makes reference to the war in heaven, though he also refers to other time periods as well. In his description of these events, John refers to this time period of forty-two months, as he makes specific reference to "time, times, and a half of time." It is important to note that the Saints at this time will have a great need for protection, not only from the serpent but also from the plagues ravaging the world.

If we take the essence of what John is trying to convey to the Saints from this chapter, our notes might resemble the following:

- Cast your mind back upon the time when the plan of salvation was being conceived and prepared. A son of the morning (red dragon) arose in opposition to God. Upon being cast out, the son of the morning convinced a third part of the host of heaven to follow after him.

- In spite of Satan's efforts, the plan of God was executed, and the mission of the Savior was successful in bringing salvation to the world.
- As persecutions arose after the establishment of the Church (in the Savior's time), God was obliged to take the Church up into heaven for 1,260 years. (The Dark Ages.)
- Now do not forget that when this initial conflict arose, Michael and his hosts fought against the dragon and his hosts. The dragon and his hosts were cast out into the earth.
- It was declared that salvation was available for the entire remaining heavenly hosts through the power and strength of Christ.
- With our valiant testimonies and willingness to sacrifice all, the atoning blood of Christ will intercede on our behalf, enabling us to overcome Satan.
- So rejoice. But beware as you pass through mortality, as the devil has great wrath because he knows that his time is short.
- Ever since he was cast into the earth, he has persecuted the Church (the Saints of God).
- The Lord will prepare your way to a place of safety to protect you for this last season (time, times, and a half a time).
- Satan will use everything at his disposal to destroy you, but God is the master, and earth is His creation. Because things are not going his way, Satan will make war with any of Heavenly Father's children that keep the commandments and have a testimony of Christ.

Though these notes are not an exact duplication of this chapter, the underlying message follows this line of thought. The idea is that through historical perspective, a message is given. Just because John refers to the past does not mean that John is now giving us a vision of the past. Remember that often in scripture the Lord requires that we seek out the message through our own sincere study, pondering, and prayer. Without the Spirit, these messages are not readily interpreted or understood. If we are humble and prayerful, the Lord will guide us.

When we consider that Satan will be given dominion during this time and that all under his power will be required to have the mark of the beast and to worship him, it is only common sense that the woman (the Church) would be taken into the wilderness and nourished from the face of the serpent. This is the period when the Saints will be away from the world, or, as some like to refer to it, "the calling out."

Without doubt, there will be those who will not heed the call or be held up on their journey and have to deal with the world. There may also be those who are, for whatever reason, unable to flee. For all people, and especially for those individuals who are not with the Saints as a group, there is a message in Revelation 13 and 14.

In chapter 13, the beast is given power and great authority for a period of forty-two months.

> *And I* stood upon the sand of the sea, and *saw a beast rise up out of the sea*, having seven heads and ten horns, and upon his horns ten crowns, and upon his heads the name of blasphemy.
>
> And the beast which I saw was like unto a leopard, and his feet were as the feet of a bear, and his mouth as the mouth of a lion: *and the dragon gave him his power, and his seat, and great authority*.
>
> And I saw one of his heads as it were wounded to death; and his deadly wound was healed: and all the world wondered after the beast.
>
> And they worshipped the dragon which gave power unto the beast: and they worshipped the beast, saying, Who is like unto the beast? Who is able to make war with him?
>
> And there was given unto him a mouth speaking great things and blasphemies; *and power was given unto him to continue forty and* two months. (Revelation 13:1–5)

The scriptures are clear that during this period of time, much power will be given to Satan.

> And it was given unto him to make war with the saints, and to overcome them: and power was given him over all kindreds, and tongues, and nations. (Revelation 13:7)

During this period of time, all people will be required to worship the beast.

And deceiveth them that dwell on the earth by the means of those miracles which he had power to do in the sight of the beast; saying to them that dwell on the earth, that they should make an image to the beast, which had the wound by a sword, and did live.

And he had power to give life unto the image of the beast, that the image of the beast should both speak, and cause that as many as would not worship the image of the beast should be killed. (Revelation 13:14–15)

And if this were not bad enough, then the mark of the beast is introduced.

And *he causeth all*, both small and great, rich and poor, free and bond, *to receive a mark in their right hand, or in their foreheads*:

And that *no man might buy or sell, save he that had the mark*, or the name of the beast, or the number of his name. (Revelation 13:16–17)

The entire world will be under martial law; all will be required to worship the beast, to buy or sell you will be required to show the mark of the beast, and so on.

A most unique thing happens in the middle of this chapter. John interrupts his vision to give perspective to the faithful, telling them that they do have a choice; maybe not the choice that they envisioned, but a choice just the same. It is almost as if the Lord is saying, for those Saints who do not flee into the wilderness or are unable to flee, pay attention to the following:

And all that dwell upon the earth shall worship him, whose names are not written in the book of life of the Lamb slain from the foundation of the world.

If any man have an ear, *let him hear*.

He that leadeth into *captivity* shall go into *captivity*: he that *killeth with sword* must be *killed with the sword*. Here is *the patience and the faith of the saints*. (Revelation 13:8–10)

The message is: Be patient in your sufferings. Those who lead others into captivity will end up in captivity, and those that kill with the sword will be killed with the sword. Those who do wicked acts will receive what is coming to them as a result of their actions.

Again, in chapter 14, we must look for the underlying message. We must understand that we are not shifting time periods but simply being given a message. Let us take notes of what the message is that John is giving us.

- The 144,000 have completed their work and stand as witnesses with the Savior. They are unique, as are their testimonies. Heaven endorses their works, and they are redeemed.
- An angel, who has the gospel to declare (this may be a reference to Moroni), has a message to deliver. Fear God—the hour of His judgment is come. Worship Him, for He is the true God.
- Another angel has a message: Babylon will fall for forcing the nations to commit sin.
- Another angel follows, saying if you worship the beast and his image, you will suffer the wrath of an impartial God exercising justice.
- Saints who are persecuted or killed for their testimonies will be rewarded and vindicated.
- The earth will be reaped, and the angels of heaven (who are to reap the earth) will thrust in their sickles and complete the work that they are commanded.

Near the end of this chapter, John interrupts his description of these events with the rest of the message that he started in the previous chapter.

> *Here is the patience of the saints*: here are they that keep the commandments of God, and the faith of Jesus.
> And I heard a voice from heaven saying unto me, Write, *Blessed are the dead which die in the Lord from henceforth*: Yea, saith the Spirit, that they may rest from their labours; and *their works do follow them*. (Revelation 14:12–13)

It seems some will be tested unto death. But they will also receive the reward for their sacrifices. We know that, for many, they will be required to give the ultimate sacrifice: to lay down their lives for the kingdom of God. Like the two prophets at Jerusalem, they will seal their testimonies with their blood.

Daniel, who talks about the fourth beast or the servant who directs Satan's dominion during the last forty-two months, also confirms these trying times.

> And the ten horns out of this kingdom are ten kings that shall arise: and another shall rise after them; and he shall be diverse from the first, and he shall subdue three kings.
>
> And he shall speak great words against the most High, and *shall wear out the saints of the most High, and think to change times and laws*: and they shall be given into his hand until a time and times and the dividing of time. (Daniel 7:24–25)

As we continue to follow John's vision of the last days, he gives us another warning in chapter 16. John describes the plagues that will come upon those who follow this servant of the adversary. Then, as we have seen in other chapters, John suddenly interrupts his commentary and gives a side note. Here, he makes a point of telling us the importance of keeping our temple covenants:

> Behold, I come as a thief. Blessed is he that watcheth, and keepeth his garments, lest he walk naked, and they see his shame. (Revelation 16:15)

It is evident that worshipping the beast and receiving his mark are only some of the concerns for the Saints in this wicked environment. To remain pure and undefiled will not be an easy task. This last warning is a timely reminder to be vigilant before the Lord comes. As the final battle approaches, the world's armies will be summoned to a final battle—the battle of Armageddon.

> And he gathered them together into a place called in the Hebrew tongue Armageddon. (Revelation 16:16)

After our review of the of the first six trumpets and vials and the warnings, we are now ready to examine the final destruction that will come upon the wicked as the advent of Jesus Christ comes upon the world.

The Seventh Trumpet and the Seventh Vial

This final trumpet and vial will announce the end of the reign of the beast. The great day of the Lord will arrive, judgment will be swift, and abominations will be removed as the earth is cleansed from iniquity.

The last angel with a trumpet announces the seventh plague as the third woe.

> The second woe is past; and, behold, the third woe cometh quickly.
> And the seventh angel sounded; and there were great voices in heaven, saying, The kingdoms of this world are become the kingdoms of our Lord, and of his Christ; and he shall reign for ever and ever. (Revelation 11:14–15)

The last angel, with the last seven plagues poured from vials, makes a similar announcement in a similar fashion.

> And the seventh angel poured out his vial into the air; and there came a great voice out of the temple of heaven, from the throne, saying, It is done. (Revelation 16:17)

These two declarations are conclusive, or final in nature. Sequentially, they occur at the exactly same time, announcing the end of the forty-two-month reign of terror by Satan. The consequence to the earth and its inhabitants is described in the following manner.

The Seventh Plague

Trumpet

> And the temple of God was opened in heaven, and there was seen in his temple the ark of his testament: and there were lightnings, and voices, and thunderings, and an earthquake, and great hail. (Revelation 11:19)

Vial

> And there were voices, and thunders, and lightnings; and there was a great earthquake, such as was not since men were upon the earth, so mighty an earthquake, and so great.
>
> And the great city was divided into three parts, and the cities of the nations fell: and great Babylon came in remembrance before God, to give unto her the cup of the wine of the fierceness of his wrath.
>
> And every island fled away, and the mountains were not found.
>
> And there fell upon men a great hail out of heaven, every stone about the weight of a talent: and men blasphemed God because of the plague of the hail; for the plague thereof was exceeding great. (Revelation 16:18–21)

The physical description of this plague is voices, thunderings, lightnings, an earthquake, and great hail. Though Revelation 16 provides greater detail than chapter 11, there is no mistake that the last plague from the angels with the seven vials and the last plague from the angels with the woes are one and the same.

This earthquake will be the greatest in the history of the planet. Elder Bruce R. McConkie taught (and this is confirmed by other scriptures that this will occur at the time of the Lord's Second Coming),

> Three natural changes in the earth—all apparently growing out of one transcendent happening—are here named [Revelation 16:17–21] as attending our Lord's Second Coming. They are:
>
> 1. Earth's land masses shall unite; islands and continents shall become one land.
>
> 2. Every valley shall be exalted and every mountain shall be made low; the rugged terrain of today shall level out into a millennial garden.
>
> 3. Such an earthquake as has never been known since man's foot was planted on this planet shall attend these changes in the earth's surface and appearance.
>
> And, fourthly, as recorded elsewhere, the great deep—presumably the Atlantic Ocean—shall return to its place in the north, 'and the earth shall be like as it was in the days before it was divided. (*Doctrinal New Testament Commentary*, 3:543)

During this earthquake, we will see the Mount of Olives split in two as the Lord sets His foot upon it, as described by Zechariah:

> And his feet shall stand in that day upon the mount of Olives, which is before Jerusalem on the east, and *the mount of Olives shall cleave in the midst thereof* toward the east and toward the west, and there shall be a very great valley; and half of the mountain shall remove toward the north, and half of it toward the south. (Zechariah 14:4)

Joseph Fielding Smith describes the scene as follows:

> All [the prophets] speak of [this day]; and when that time comes, the Lord is going to come out of His hiding place. You can see what a terrible condition it is going to be; and the Jews besieged, not only in Jerusalem but, of course, throughout Palestine are in the siege; and when they are about to go under, then the Lord comes. There will be the great earthquake. The earthquake will not be only in Palestine. There will not be merely the separation of the Mount of Olives, to form a valley that the Jews may escape, but the whole earth is going to be shaken. There will be some dreadful things take place, and some great changes are going to take place, and that you will find written in the book of Ezekiel (38:17–23). [Joseph Fielding Smith, *The Signs of the Times* (Salt Lake City: Deseret Book, 1970), 170]

As the Mount of Olives is split in two, the Jews will flee from the armies of Gog.

> And ye shall flee to the valley of the mountains; for the valley of the mountains shall reach unto Azal: yea, ye shall flee, like as ye fled from before the earthquake in the days of Uzziah king of Judah: and the Lord my God shall come, and all the saints with thee. (Zechariah 14:5)

At this point, the Jews will encounter the Savior. This meeting is described in a revelation given to the Prophet Joseph Smith.

> Then shall the arm of the Lord fall upon the nations.
> And then shall the Lord set his foot upon this mount, and it shall cleave in twain, and the earth shall tremble, and reel to and fro, and the heavens also shall shake.

And the Lord shall utter his voice, and all the ends of the earth shall hear it; and the nations of the earth shall mourn, and they that have laughed shall see their folly.

And calamity shall cover the mocker, and the scorner shall be consumed; and they that have watched for iniquity shall be hewn down and cast into the fire.

And then shall the Jews look upon me and say: what are these wounds in thine hands and in thy feet?

Then shall they know that I am the Lord; for I will say unto them: These wounds are the wounds with which I was wounded in the house of my friends. I am he who was lifted up. I am Jesus that was crucified. I am the son of God.

And then shall they weep because of their iniquities; then shall they lament because they persecuted their king. (D&C 45:47–53)

There will then be a great hailstorm, with fire and brimstone that will fall upon the armies of Gog and upon the inhabitants of the earth.

And it shall come to pass at the same time when Gog shall come against the land of Israel, saith the Lord God, that my fury shall come up in my face.

For in my jealousy and in the fire of my wrath have I spoken, Surely in that day there shall be a great shaking in the land of Israel;

So that the fishes of the sea, and the fowls of the heaven, and the beasts of the field, and all creeping things that creep upon the earth, and all the men that are upon the face of the earth, shall shake at my presence, and the mountains shall be thrown down, and the steep places shall fall, and every wall shall fall to the ground.

And I will call for a sword against him throughout all my mountains, saith the Lord God: every man's sword shall be against his brother.

And I will plead against him with pestilence and with blood; and I will rain upon him, and upon his bands, and upon the many people that are with him, an overflowing rain, and *great hailstones*, fire, and brimstone.

Thus will I magnify myself, and sanctify myself; and I will be known in the eyes of many nations, and they shall know that I am the Lord. (Ezekiel 38:18–23)

The rain of fire and brimstone in verse 22 is in reference to the day of burning, when many will be left as stubble. In Revelation 18, we read that Babylon (meaning the buildings, factories, cities, or, in other words, material wealth that constitute Babylon) will go up in smoke, and the wicked rulers will be witness to it.

> Therefore shall her plagues come in one day, death, and mourning, and famine; and she shall be utterly burned with fire: for strong is the Lord God who judgeth her.
>
> And the kings of the earth, who have committed fornication and lived deliciously with her, shall bewail her, and lament for her, when they shall see the smoke of her burning. (Revelation 18:8–9)

The destruction of the wicked could be in battle, by great hail, by fire and brimstone, by scourge, by earthquake, by oceans being displaced, or many other events. Many of the wicked that remain will become prey to the lost tribes as they return to seek their inheritance.

The Destruction of Babylon

Revelation 18 describes Babylon's destruction and the mourning of the rich men of the world who see the loss of their earthly possessions. The first part of the chapter sets the stage and provides a warning to the Saints to avoid the wickedness of Babylon.

> And after these things I saw another angel come down from heaven, *having great power; and the earth was lightened with his glory.*
>
> And he cried mightily with a strong voice, saying, Babylon the great is fallen, is fallen, and is become the habitation of devils, and the hold of every foul spirit, and a cage of every unclean and hateful bird.
>
> For all nations have drunk of the wine of the wrath of her fornication, and the kings of the earth have committed fornication with her, and the merchants of the earth are waxed rich through the abundance of her delicacies. (Revelation 18:1–3)

The description of this messenger is unique, in that his presence illuminates the earth and that he has great power. Either this angel is accompanying the Savior in His Second Coming, or this portrayal of a heavenly being is meant to describe the Savior as He comes to the earth.

John then gives a warning to the Saints:

> And I heard another voice from heaven, saying, Come out of her, my people, that ye be not partakers of her sins, and that ye receive not of her plagues. (Revelation 18:4)

Here again, we are reminded that if we do not partake of Babylon, we will not receive her plagues. We are expressly commanded to come out of Babylon.

The rest of the chapter creates a vivid mental picture of the consequences of Babylon, showing why we should come out of it. There can be no mistake as to the speed with which all this destruction takes place. The time frame "in one hour" is repeated three times (verses 10, 17, and 19). Truly this will come upon the people as a thief in the night. There is no way for the wicked to protect against such devastation.

For the lands of the world to come together and the mountains to be laid low, it would take longer than five minutes. If an event of this magnitude, bringing the continents together, takes only an hour, it would seem that nothing much would be left standing. It takes six hours to fly across the Atlantic in a plane. This is the reason why the majority of the building of the New Jerusalem will most likely begin after the lands are brought together.

To give a clear picture of how devastating this will be, let us analyze the rest of this chapter:

> Standing afar off for the fear of her torment, saying, Alas, alas, that great city Babylon, that mighty city! for in one hour is thy judgment come.
>
> And the merchants of the earth shall weep and mourn over her; for no man buyeth their merchandise any more:
>
> The merchandise of gold, and silver, and precious stones, and of pearls, and fine linen, and purple, and silk, and scarlet, and all thyine wood, and all manner vessels of ivory, and all manner vessels of most precious wood, and of brass, and iron, and marble,

And cinnamon, and odours, and ointments, and frankincense, and wine, and oil, and fine flour, and wheat, and beasts, and sheep, and horses, and chariots, and slaves, and souls of men.

And the fruits that thy soul lusted after are departed from thee, and all things which were dainty and goodly are departed from thee, and thou shalt find them no more at all. [Basically there is no more merchandise to sell or to buy.]

The merchants of these things, which were made rich by her, shall stand afar off for the fear of her torment, weeping and wailing. . . .

For in one hour so great riches is come to nought. And every shipmaster, and all the company in ships, and sailors, and as many as trade by sea, stood afar off. . . .

And they cast dust on their heads, and cried, weeping and wailing, saying, Alas, alas, that great city, wherein were made rich all that had ships in the sea by reason of her costliness! for in one hour is she made desolate. . . .

And the voice of harpers, and musicians, and of pipers, and trumpeters, shall be heard no more at all in thee; and no craftsman, of whatsoever craft he be, shall be found any more in thee; and the sound of a millstone shall be heard no more at all in thee. (Revelation 18:10–15, 17, 19, 22)

There will be no factories, no ships, no warehouses, no airplanes, no exotic vacations, no malls, no electricity, no beautiful summer cottages, no highways, no cars, and no personal belongings. Everything—absolutely everything—will be destroyed. The institutions of mankind will be destroyed: the banks, insurance companies, stock exchange, Medicare, social assistance, local PTA, and governments. Even the land you thought you owned will no longer be recognizable, or even in the same geographical location.

This is borne out in following statement:

And a mighty angel took up a stone like a great millstone, and cast it into the sea, saying, Thus with violence shall that great city Babylon be thrown down, and shall be found no more at all. (Revelation 18:21)

In verse 23, we see some perilous insights into our current state of affairs, which will continue to degenerate as time ticks on.

> And the light of a candle shall shine no more at all in thee; and the voice of the bridegroom and of the bride shall be heard no more at all in thee: for thy merchants were the great men of the earth; for by thy sorceries were all nations deceived. (Revelation 18:23)

These are the consequences heaped upon Babylon. The final state of Babylon is also mentioned. The Spirit of the Lord will withdraw, and there will be no more opportunities for forgiveness; those of Babylon will have purchased their destiny from the men of earth, instead of the Lord. We also gain insight into the business practices of Babylon. Those of the earth will have deceived the nations by their sorceries—implying not just trickery and deceit, but also poisoning.

We see evidence of this implied poisoning in many aspects of life: the environment, food, medications, entertainment, education, societal norms, and so on. We are surrounded and subject to physical and spiritual poisoning. Is it any wonder that the Lord warns the Saints to come out of Babylon?

It is our obligation to be aware that many of our everyday practices fall into this category. We are being deceived by the people of the earth to follow poor business practices, environmental practices, manufacturing practices, farming practices, medical practices, and so on. Some of these practices are cleverly deceptive, driven by money, and do not follow the plan that the Lord has in mind for care and keeping of His children or this earth.

Because we are not commanded in all things, the Lord expects us to use our common sense and discernment in how we participate in these practices. As individuals, we must inform ourselves so we can understand and be warned of the consequences of the activities that we engage in.

The Lord laid out a pattern for us in Doctrine and Covenants 89. He started off with a warning:

> In consequence of evils and designs which do and will exist in the hearts of conspiring men in the last days, I have warned you, and forewarn you, by giving unto you this word of wisdom by revelation. (Revelation 89:4)

He then revealed important information, among other things, about what we should and should not put in our bodies. The Lord, however, does not command us in all aspects of our individual lives. In Section 58, He revealed,

> For behold, it is not meet that I should command in all things; for he that is compelled in all things, the same is a slothful and not a wise servant; wherefore he receiveth no reward.
>
> Verily I say, men should be anxiously engaged in a good cause, and do many things of their own free will, and bring to pass much righteousness;
>
> For the power is in them, wherein they are agents unto themselves. And inasmuch as men do good they shall in nowise lose their reward. (D&C 58:26–28)

While genetically altered foods and grains can be resistant to disease and adaptive to varying climate conditions, they often lack nutrition and reproductive ability. By not producing our own seed, we lose this skill, have less nutrition, and may find it difficult to have quality seed when hard times come upon us.

Much of modern medicine has allowed us physical blessings that we might otherwise not have had. It also has its drawbacks, as some medications have serious side effects. The billion-dollar pharmaceutical companies are driven by profit, and some companies have been less than forthright in their practices. By pursuing dollars instead of health, they have left many to suffer the devastating consequences of their actions. Though some of the natural medicines may not cure all of our ills, the skill in their administration may be essential in times of trial, when access to modern remedies is not available for extended periods of time.

While the great industrial machine has produced many of our modern conveniences, including electrical power, it has left its mark on the environment. Chemical contaminations from factories and other events (such as the "Fukashima" disaster) pollute our world. The people, plants, and animals suffer the consequences. Just as food storage will be essential, so will the tools and the written handbooks be—to help us produce the products when they are no longer available on the store shelves.

Human beings were given the responsibility to look after the earth. Unfortunately, the men and women in this world do not always consult Heavenly Father in developing technologies.

We are commanded to pray over our sick, our gardens, and our work. If this had truly been mankind's process, then perhaps we would have been granted more wisdom in being led to better ways to grow our food, to heal our sick, and to manufacture our goods. Until we pursue enlightenment from the Lord, we do not know what wisdom God can impart. For example, the Lord says,

> And again, verily I say unto you, all wholesome herbs God hath
> ordained for the constitution, nature, and use of man. (D&C 89:10)

In speaking about the founder of the Thomsonian Botanical Cure and his practice of herbal medicine, Joseph Smith said, "Thomson was as much inspired to bring forth his principle of practice according to the dignity and importance of it as he [Joseph] was to introduce the gospel" (John Heinerman, *Joseph Smith and Herbal Medicine*, 11).

In the final verse of Revelation 18, we see the full extent of the sin of murder laid upon Babylon, or upon he who first taught this wickedness to Cain. In the end, Babylon is, among other things, stained with the blood of the world.

> And in her was found the blood of prophets, and of saints, and of
> all that were slain upon the earth. (Revelation 18:24)

The plagues, the earthquakes, and the hail are part of the destruction of Babylon. This day is also referred to as a day of burning.

A Day of Burning

To most of us, "a day of burning" invokes images of fire. However, a day of burning, like many things in the scriptures, has more than one meaning.

As a consequence of wickedness, a day of burning is also known as a day of destruction or a day of wrath.

Behold, vengeance cometh speedily upon the inhabitants of the earth, a day of wrath, a day of burning, a day of desolation, of weeping, of mourning, and of lamentation; and as a whirlwind it shall come upon all the face of the earth, saith the Lord. (D&C 112:24)

As an event, the day of burning is also described.

Behold, now it is called today until the coming of the Son of Man, and verily it is a day of sacrifice, and a day for the tithing of my people; for he that is tithed shall not be burned at his coming.

For after today cometh the burning—this is speaking after the manner of the Lord—for verily I say, tomorrow all the proud and they that do wickedly shall be as stubble; and I will burn them up, for I am the Lord of Hosts; and I will not spare any that remain in Babylon. (D&C 64:23–24)

Looking at this in terms of time sequence, "today" would be from the time this revelation was given until the coming of the Son of Man. After this is the day of burning—"after today cometh the burning."

A conference talk discussing this scripture offers some insight into the meaning of this event:

What does that mean? Does it mean that if a man will not pay his tithing, that the Lord is going to send a ball of fire down from heaven and burn him up? No; the Lord does not do that way. The Lord works on natural principles. This is what it means, if I read correctly: a man who ignores the express command of the Lord, by failing to pay his tithing, it means that the spirit of the Lord will withdraw from him; it means that the power of the priesthood will withdraw from that man, if he continues in the spirit of neglect to do his duty. He will drift away into darkness, gradually but surely, until finally (mark you) he will lift up his eyes among the wicked. That is where he will finally land; and then when the destruction comes and when the burning comes he will be among the wicked and will be destroyed; while those who observe the law will be found among the righteous, and they will be preserved. There is a God in heaven, and He had promised to shield and protect them. I tell you there is a day of burning, a day of destruction coming upon the wicked. (Rudger J. Clawson, in Conference Report, October 1913, 59)

To understand the timing of the actual event of the burning, we can refer to the Doctrine and Covenants. Here, we see that, even as the Lord returns, the process of destruction will be one of wrath and desolation as well as burning.

> He shall command the great deep, and it shall be driven back into the north countries, and the islands shall become one land;
>
> And the land of Jerusalem and the land of Zion shall be turned back into their own place, and the earth shall be like as it was in the days before it was divided.
>
> And the Lord, even the Savior, shall stand in the midst of his people, and shall reign over all flesh.
>
> And they who are in the north countries shall come in remembrance before the Lord; and their prophets shall hear his voice, and shall no longer stay themselves; and they shall smite the rocks, and the ice shall flow down at their presence.
>
> And an highway shall be cast up in the midst of the great deep. Their enemies shall become a prey unto them. (D&C 133:23–28)

As the lost tribes return, the wicked stragglers who remain after the main battle and survive the earthquakes and the abomination of desolation will fall victim to this returning group of Saints as they help work clean up for the Lord during this time of destruction.

In Revelation, we read,

> Therefore shall her plagues come in one day, death, and mourning, and famine; and she shall be utterly burned with fire: for strong is the Lord God who judgeth her. (Revelation 18:8)

So if some of the wicked are not overcome by one of the plagues (including the abomination of desolation) or by death (which could come by earthquake, war, extreme hail, or the return of the lost tribes), then they will mourn, starve, and finally burn. There is no escape for the wicked.

In addition to the day of burning, there will be times during the last forty-two months, prior to the Second Coming, when there will be actual fire:

And the fourth angel poured out his vial upon the sun; and power was given unto him to scorch men with fire. (Revelation 16:18)

Here, we see that before the wicked are entirely swept off and burned, they will see the destruction of their world, including the burning of all that they have—their worldly possessions gone up in fire.

And the kings of the earth, who have committed fornication and lived deliciously with her, shall bewail her, and lament for her, when they shall see the smoke of her burning,

Standing afar off for the fear of her torment, saying, Alas, alas, that great city Babylon, that mighty city! for in one hour is thy judgment come. (Revelation 18:9–10)

Here is a likely scenario of how these events will come to pass:

And there shall be silence in heaven for the space of half an hour; and immediately after shall the curtain of heaven be unfolded, as a scroll is unfolded after it is rolled up, and the face of the Lord shall be unveiled;

And the saints that are upon the earth, who are alive, shall be quickened and be caught up to meet him.

Here, Christ has received the keys from the gathering at Adam-ondi-Ahman and is preparing to reign down destruction upon the earth, as the judgment has been set.

And they who have slept in their graves shall come forth, for their graves shall be opened; and they also shall be caught up to meet him in the midst of the pillar of heaven—

They are Christ's, the first fruits, they who shall descend with him first, and they who are on the earth and in their graves, who are first caught up to meet him; and all this by the voice of the sounding of the trump of the angel of God. . . .

And this shall be the sound of his trump, saying to all people, both in heaven and in earth, and that are under the earth—for every ear shall hear it, and every knee shall bow, and every tongue shall confess, while they hear the sound of the trump, saying: Fear God, and give glory to him who sitteth upon the throne, forever and ever; for the hour of his judgment is come.

This is when the great earthquake will happen, the lands coming together as a highway is cast up out of the great deep and the mighty hail destroys the great Babylon in one hour. Elsewhere on the earth, the wicked will be burned as stubble, the final cleansing taking place.

> And again, another angel shall sound his trump, which is the sixth angel, saying: She is fallen who made all nations drink of the wine of the wrath of her fornication; she is fallen, is fallen! (D&C 88:95–98, 104–5)

Then the majority of the destruction will be complete, and the lost tribes will return, destroying the wicked who remain. Others will be dying from exposure to the abomination of desolation and other disasters. The prophet Joseph Fielding Smith provides some perspective on why the wicked cannot remain:

> The world is the people who dwell upon the face of the earth, and when Christ comes there will be an end to the world, this world, and then we will get a new earth and a new heaven just as Isaiah declares in the 65th chapter, beginning with the 17th verse, so you can look it up. The lord will give us a new earth, a cleansed earth, a restored earth, the one we sing about and preach about; as stated in the tenth Article of Faith, the earth will be renewed and receive its paradisiacal glory, cleansed from wickedness. (Joseph Fielding Smith, *The Signs of the Times*, 122–23)

He also said, in an earlier part of his book,

> You read the first verses of Malachi. He tells you that the inhabitants of the earth will be burned when Christ comes and all the wicked who are not destroyed before he comes shall be as stubble and they will be consumed. They can't stay here. Why? Because this earth is going to pass from the telestial to a terrestrial order. That is why. It will be a terrestrial world for a thousand years, and that's why death is suspended . . . the inhabitants of the earth will have a sort of translation. They will be transferred to a condition of the terrestrial order, and so they will have power over disease and they will have power to live until they get a certain age and then they will die. (Joseph Fielding Smith, *The Signs of the Times*, 42)

And in the Doctrine and Covenants:

> And again, another angel shall sound his trump, which is the seventh angel, saying: It is finished; it is finished! The Lamb of God hath overcome and trodden the wine-press alone, even the wine-press of the fierceness of the wrath of Almighty God. (D&C 88:106)

The wicked will be destroyed from off the face of the earth, and we will then be ready to proceed with the ushering in of the millennial reign, as the earth undergoes terrestrial changes and the kingdom of Christ is established.

> And then shall the angels be crowned with the glory of his might, and the saints shall be filled with his glory, and receive their inheritance and be made equal with him. (D&C 88:107)

In our discussions of this time period, we have focused on the warnings and destruction that will come to the earth. Hopefully, we now have a better idea of what to expect. There are also other events in this time that we need to examine in more detail. These events are more uplifting and carry a different message. In the next chapter, we will turn our attention to the how events like the building of the New Jerusalem, the mission of the 144,000, and the gathering at Adam-ondi-Ahman can be clarified and how they fit into the sequence of last days.

Summary Points

- This is when the Lord will prepare the earth for His coming by cleansing the earth and binding Satan.
- The abomination of desolation and its scourge will be released.
- Plagues will be poured out upon the earth.
- The Church will flee into the wilderness (meaning called out into a secure location).
- The mark of the beast will be actively enforced.
- The two prophets in Jerusalem will protect the city.
- Anti-Christs and false prophets will be at large.
- The battle of Armageddon will take place.

- At Adam-ondi-Ahman, priesthood keys will be returned to Christ.
- The Saints will be caught up to meet Christ.
- An earthquake will occur of monumental proportions, the lands become one.
- Hail from heaven will weigh one talent per stone.
- The wicked who remain will be burned, and Christ will return triumphantly to the earth.
- The lost tribes will come back, destroying the wicked who remain.
- The earth will be transformed into a terrestrial body.
- The City of Enoch will rejoin the world.

CHAPTER 5: EVENTS CLARIFIED

The Lost Tribes and the 144,000

*T*here has always been an air of mystery and intrigue when we talk about the lost tribes of Israel—a group of people who have been led away into the north. Only some of these ten tribes were led away. The remnant from these tribes were dispersed among the nations of the earth and scattered to and fro upon the isles of the sea. Those from the tribes of Joseph and Judah were also scattered among all nations. The references to these various groups are as follows: the lost tribes, the lost ten tribes, the children of Israel, the outcasts of Israel, the root of Jesse, the remnant of His people, the seed of Abraham, the other tribes of Israel, other sheep, the house of Jacob, our seed, the remnant of our seed, and so on.

With all the variations of names, main groups, remnants, and possible locations where they are, have been, and will be, is there any wonder that there could be some confusion and uncertainty as to who the scriptures may be referring to, or which group will be gathered where and when.

In reference to the "lost tribes" that were led away into the north country, we read,

> Neither at any time hath the Father given me commandment that I should tell unto them concerning the other tribes of the house of Israel, whom the Father hath led away out of the land. (3 Nephi 15:15)

> And verily, verily, I say unto you that I have other sheep, which are not of this land, neither of the land of Jerusalem, neither in any parts of that land round about whither I have been to minister.
>
> For they of whom I speak are they who have not as yet heard my voice; neither have I at any time manifested myself unto them.
>
> But I have received a commandment of the Father that I shall go unto them, and that they shall hear my voice, and shall be numbered among my sheep, that there may be one fold and one shepherd; therefore I go to show myself unto them. (3 Nephi 16:1–3)

We know of their existence and that they are not known to the world as we know them. There is no historical information, other than the scriptures and the writings of the Prophet Joseph Smith, that references the Savior visiting such a group. If we examine our world's history, I am not aware of any record or even folklore of the resurrected Lord appearing to any group apart from the Nephites. There are, however, references to the lost tribes. Some of the explorers, upon reaching the Americas or visiting the Andes, thought that the native people were part of the lost tribes. There have also been reports of lost civilizations. From the Doctrine and Covenants, we learn that this specific group will return at the Second Coming.

> He shall command the great deep, and it shall be driven back into the north countries, and the islands shall become one land;
>
> And the land of Jerusalem and the land of Zion shall be turned back into their own place, and the earth shall be like as it was in the days before it was divided.

And the Lord, even the *Savior, shall stand in the midst of his people, and shall reign over all flesh.*

And *they who are in the north countries shall come in remembrance before the Lord; and their prophets shall hear his voice, and shall no longer stay themselves*; and they shall smite the rocks, and the ice shall flow down at their presence.

And an highway shall be cast up in the midst of the great deep.

Their enemies shall become a prey unto them,

And in the barren deserts there shall come forth pools of living water; and the parched ground shall no longer be a thirsty land.

And they shall bring forth their rich treasures unto the children of Ephraim, my servants. (D&C 133:23–30)

Joseph Fielding Smith said,

Of these lost tribes the Prophet Joseph Smith stated during a conference of the Church in June, 1831 that "John the Revelator was then among the ten tribes of Israel" and was working "to prepare them for their return from their long dispersion." [Joseph Fielding Smith, *Essentials in Church History* (Salt Lake City: Deseret News Press, 1992), 126]

Only some of these tribes were led away as a group. Those who remained in Assyria were scattered among the nations, with those who had either eluded capture or had intermingled with other nations. It should also be noted that the Levites, in carrying out their priesthood duties, were among all of the tribes. There remains a significant population of all of these tribes in the world today. The Lord noted this distinction on His visit to the Nephites.

And I command you that ye shall write these sayings after I am gone, that if it so be that my *people at Jerusalem*, they who have seen me and been with me in my ministry, do not ask the Father in my name, that they may receive a knowledge of you by the Holy Ghost, and also of the *other tribes whom they know not of*, that these sayings which ye shall write shall be kept and shall be manifested unto the Gentiles, that through the fulness of the Gentiles, *the remnant of their seed, who shall be scattered forth upon the face of the earth* because of their unbelief, may be brought in, or may be brought to a knowledge of me, their Redeemer.

And then will I gather them in from the four quarters of the earth; and then will I fulfil the covenant which the Father hath made unto all the people of the house of Israel. (3 Nephi 16:4–5)

It is important to make this distinction to understand the unfolding of God's work in these last days. During the sixth seal, the Lord will seal 144,000 of His servants to do a great work. This group of 144,000 is to be composed of, according to John, twelve thousand from twelve different tribes.

As this event will happen prior to the Second Coming, we know that the lost tribes have not yet returned. This is supported by revelation that was given to the Prophet Joseph when inquiring about the 144,000:

Q. What are we to understand by sealing the one hundred and forty-four thousand, out of all the tribes of Israel—twelve thousand out of every tribe?

A. We are to understand that those who are sealed are high priests, ordained unto the holy order of God, to administer the everlasting gospel; for they are they who are *ordained out of every nation, kindred, tongue, and people,* by the angels to whom is given power over the nations of the earth, to bring as many as will come to the church of the Firstborn. (D&C 77:11)

Therefore, the ranks of this group of the Lord's anointed will consist of those of the remnant of the lost tribes who remained behind, were scattered, and were brought back into the covenant through missionary efforts. President Joseph Fielding Smith made it clear that a majority of the members of the Church today are descendants of Israel and thus of Abraham:

The Lord said he would scatter Israel among the Gentile nations, and by doing so he would bless the Gentile nations with the blood of Abraham. Today we are preaching the gospel in the world and we are gathering out, according to the revelations given to Isaiah, Jeremiah, and other prophets, the scattered sheep of the House of Israel. These scattered sheep are coming forth mixed with Gentile blood from their Gentile forefathers.

Under all the circumstances it is very possible that the majority, almost without exception, of *those who come into the Church in this dispensation have the blood of two or more of the tribes of Israel* as well as the blood of the Gentiles. [Joseph Fielding Smith, *Answers to Gospel Questions*, 5 vols. (Salt Lake City: Deseret Book, 1957–66), 3:63.]

In referencing the question of becoming part of the house of Israel, President Brigham Young stated,

If any of the Gentiles will believe, we will lay our hands upon them that they may receive the Holy Ghost, and the Lord will make them of the house of Israel. They will be broken off from the wild olive tree, and be grafted into the good and tame olive tree, and will partake of its sap and fatness. . . .

It is so with the House of Israel and the Gentile nations; if the Gentiles are grafted into the good olive tree they will partake of its root and fatness. [Brigham Young, *Journal of Discourses*, 26 vols. (London: Latter-day Saints' Book Depot, 1854–86), 2:269]

Joseph Fielding Smith gave the following explanation on the same topic:

Every person who embraces the gospel becomes of the house of Israel. In other words, they become members of the chosen lineage, or Abraham's children through Isaac and Jacob unto whom the promises were made. The great majority of those who become members of the Church are literal descendants of Abraham through Ephraim, son of Joseph.

Those who are not literal descendants of Abraham and Israel must become such, and when they are baptized and confirmed they are grafted into the tree and are entitled to all the rights and privileges as heirs. [Joseph Fielding Smith. *Doctrines of Salvation*, 3 vols. (Salt Lake City: Bookcraft, 1954–56), 3:246]

As the gospel continues to spread throughout all the earth, these members of the house of Israel will be gathered in. We see patriarchal blessings that declare lineage from all of the tribes of Israel. It is priesthood holders from the remnant of these tribes who were scattered that will be gathered and set apart—who will form the 144,000. The lost tribes as a group will not return until after Christ comes to the earth.

This group will not be part of the 144,000; the 144,000 will be called and set apart during the sixth seal, at least fifteen to twenty-five years prior to the Second Coming. As part of their mission, the 144,000 will be witnesses of the rejection of the gospel by the world prior to the Lord's return.

> When the Lamb shall stand upon Mount Zion, and with him a hundred and forty-four thousand, having his Father's name written on their foreheads.
>
> Wherefore, prepare ye for the coming of the Bridegroom; go ye, go ye out to meet him. (D&C 133:18–19)

According to John, when Jesus Christ and the 144,000 stand on Mount Zion, we are to prepare for His coming and go out to meet him.

The word *prepare* indicates time; how much time, we are not sure. This also lets us know that the 144,000 are with Christ prior to His Second Coming and prior to the return of the lost tribes.

> And I looked, and, lo, a Lamb stood on the mount Sion, and with him an hundred forty and four thousand, having his Father's name written in their foreheads.
>
> And I heard a voice from heaven, as the voice of many waters, and as the voice of a great thunder: and I heard the voice of harpers harping with their harps:
>
> And they sung as it were a new song before the throne, and before the four beasts, and the elders: and no man could learn that song but the hundred and forty and four thousand, which were redeemed from the earth. (Revelation 14:1–3)

When *the Lamb shall stand upon Mount Zion, and with him a hundred and forty-four thousand,* having his Father's name written on their foreheads.

Wherefore, prepare ye for the coming of the Bridegroom; go ye, go ye out to meet him.

For behold, he shall stand upon the mount of Olivet, and upon the mighty ocean, even the great deep, and upon the islands of the sea, and upon the land of Zion.

And he shall utter his voice out of Zion, and he shall speak from Jerusalem, and his voice shall be heard among all people;

And it shall be a voice as the voice of many waters, and as the voice of a great thunder, *which shall break down the mountains, and the valleys shall not be found.*

He shall command the great deep, and it shall be driven back into the north countries, and the islands shall become one land. (D&C 133:18–23)

The rest of Revelation 14 talks about various warnings to the earth, and then "the wine press was trodden." In conclusion, it only makes sense that the 144,000 on Mount Zion happens after the peoples of the world entirely reject the gospel prior to the return of the lost tribes. Thus with their mission accomplished, these faithful high priests glory with God and sing the song that those who have not done their works cannot sing. This would be some time prior to the time of the judgment spoken of in Revelation 11:18, just before the Savior comes.

As a point of interest, the composition of the 144,000 does not mention those of the tribe of Dan.

And I heard the number of them which were sealed: and there were sealed an hundred and forty and four thousand of all the tribes of the children of Israel.

Of the tribe of *Juda* were sealed twelve thousand. Of the tribe of *Reuben* were sealed twelve thousand. Of the tribe of *Gad* were sealed twelve thousand.

Of the tribe of *Aser* were sealed twelve thousand. Of the tribe of *Nepthalim* were sealed twelve thousand. Of the tribe of *Manasses* were sealed twelve thousand.

Of the tribe of *Simeon* were sealed twelve thousand. Of the tribe of *Levi* were sealed twelve thousand. Of the tribe of *Issachar* were sealed twelve thousand.

Of the tribe of *Zabulon* were sealed twelve thousand. Of the tribe of *Joseph* were sealed twelve thousand. Of the tribe of *Benjamin* were sealed twelve thousand. (Revelation 7:4–8)

Adam-ondi-Ahman

Adam-ondi-Ahman is the name of the valley where Adam gathered his righteous posterity prior to his death and bestowed upon them his last blessing.

Here, the Lord ministered comfort unto him, calling him a prince over the nations forever. Being filled with the Holy Ghost, Adam predicted what would happen to his posterity unto the latest generation.

This was recorded in the book of Enoch and will be brought forth at an appropriate time (see D&C 107:53–57).

> Spring Hill is named by the Lord Adam-ondi-Ahman, because, said he, it is the place where Adam shall come to visit his people, or the Ancient of Days shall sit, as spoken of by Daniel the prophet. (D&C 116:1)

This priesthood council will attend to matters concerning the destiny of the earth. It is here that Christ will receive the keys from the various dispensations as stewardships report. It is a hallowed gathering that will take place unbeknownst to the world at large. It is also to be a reward to the faithful Saints who have endured through the events of final forty-two months prior to the Second Coming, which this gathering precedes.

Daniel describes how and when this event is to unfold:

> I beheld till the thrones were cast down, and the Ancient of days did sit, whose garment was white as snow, and the hair of his head like the pure wool: his throne was like the fiery flame, and his wheels as burning fire. (Daniel 7:9)

It is clear that Adam will not come until all thrones are cast down, or in other words until there are no more dominions that have power over the people of the earth. The greatest dominion, of course, is the last dominion that is controlled by Satan through the anti-Christ. This throne is pure evil, causing people to worship the beast under pain of death and letting wickedness reign without bounds. So evil will be the times that the Saints will flee into the wilderness to be protected by God against the rest of the world.

> And there was given unto him a mouth speaking great things and blasphemies; and *power was given unto him* to continue forty and two months. . . .
>
> And it was given unto him *to make war with the saints, and to overcome them*: and power was given him *over all kindreds, and tongues, and nations.* (Revelation 13:5, 7)

> And *to the woman were given two wings of a great eagle, that she might fly into the wilderness,* into her place, *where she is nourished for a time, and times, and half a time, from the face of the serpent.* (Revelation 12:14)

Adam's visit to this sacred meeting is part of the judgment.

> A fiery stream issued and came forth from before him: thousand thousands ministered unto him, and ten thousand times ten thousand stood before him: the judgment was set, and the books were opened. (Daniel 7:10)

The word *judgment* in this verse has a footnote that refers us to Revelation 11:18 and to the Topical Guide, under the entry "Judgment, the Last." If we read in Revelation 11, we see that before this judgment, the two prophets who die in the streets of Jerusalem will be resurrected and taken up into heaven. There is a great earthquake, and great voices from heaven declare that the kingdoms of the world will become the kingdoms of God.

> And after three days and an half the Spirit of life from God entered into them, and they stood upon their feet; and great fear fell upon them which saw them.

> And they heard a great voice from heaven saying unto them,
> Come up hither. And they ascended up to heaven in a cloud; and
> their enemies beheld them.
>
> And the same hour was there a great earthquake. . . .
>
> And there were great voices in heaven, saying, The kingdoms of
> this world are become the kingdoms of our Lord, and of his Christ;
> and he shall reign for ever and ever. (Revelation 11:11–13, 15)

The timing of this great judgment now becomes apparent. It comes in the aftermath of the great siege of Jerusalem, where the holy city shall be tread under foot for forty-two months (see Revelation 11:2). Daniel confirms that, in fact, these kingdoms will be taken away.

> I beheld then because of the voice of the great words which the horn
> spake: I beheld even till the beast was slain, and his body destroyed,
> and given to the burning flame.
>
> As concerning the rest of the beasts, they *had their dominion
> taken away*: yet their lives were prolonged for a season and time.
>
> I saw in the night visions, and, behold, one like the Son of man
> came with the clouds of heaven, and came to the Ancient of days,
> and they brought him near before him.
>
> And there was given him dominion, and glory, and a kingdom,
> that all people, nations, and languages, should serve him: his domin-
> ion is an everlasting dominion, which shall not pass away, and his
> kingdom that which shall not be destroyed. (Daniel 7:11–14)

Here again, we see that the beast will be destroyed and that the other beasts have their dominion taken away. The Savior Himself will come to this great gathering to receive the keys of the dispensations. This echoes the words of John in his record:

> And the nations were angry, and thy wrath is come, *and the time
> of the dead, that they should be judged*, and that thou shouldest give
> reward unto thy servants the prophets, and to the saints, and them
> that fear thy name, small and great; and shouldest destroy them
> which destroy the earth. (Revelation 11:18)

We see that the dead will be ready for judgment and that the Savior will need to give reward to the prophets, the Saints, and those who fear him. It will be time for Him to go to see the ancient of days and visit His people in a sacred meeting prior to His coming in glory.

Daniel tells us of the intent of Satan and his dominion on earth and how Satan's reign will end:

> And he shall speak great words against the most High, and *shall wear out the saints* of the most High, and *think to change times and laws*: and they shall be given into his hand *until a time and times and the dividing of time.*
>
> But the judgment shall sit, *and they shall take away his dominion, to consume and to destroy it unto the end.*
>
> And the kingdom and dominion, and the greatness of the kingdom under the whole heaven, shall be given to the people of the saints of the most High*, whose kingdom is an everlasting kingdom, and all dominions shall serve and obey him. (Daniel 7:25–27)

Satan's idea is to change the times and laws to wear out the Saints. He wants to rule and bring everything into submission. This is only a temporary situation.

We can also clarify the timing of Adam-ondi-Ahman. It takes place at the end of the forty-two-month period connected to the end of Satan's dominion and the judgment.In addition to visiting the Saints at Adam-ondi-Ahman, the Savior will set up an everlasting kingdom where peace will reign and the evils of the telestial world will be nonexistent—where the greatness of the kingdom will be given to the Saints as part of the reward, as declared from heaven (see Revelation 11:18).

We know from the prophet Joseph Fielding Smith that not all of the Saints will attend this gathering. Even the following scripture qualifies the attendees:

> Thy servants the prophets, and to the saints, and to them that fear thy name. (Revelation 11:18)

The phrase *them that fear thy name* is indicative of a God-fearing person, or one who honors God and lives the gospel in a sincere manner.

Joseph Fielding Smith also said,

> When this gathering is held, the world will not know of it; the members of the Church at large will not know of it, yet it shall be preparatory to the coming in the clouds of glory of our Savior Jesus Christ as the Prophet Joseph Smith has said.
>
> The world cannot know of it. The Saints cannot know of it—except those who officially shall be called into this council—for it shall precede the coming of Jesus Christ as a thief in the night, unbeknown to all the world. [Joseph Fielding Smith, *The Way to Perfection*, Ninth Edition (Salt Lake City: Genealogical Society of The Church of Jesus Christ of Latter-day Saints, 1951), 287–91]

As God prepares for the destruction to come, we get a glimpse of how this is to come about.

> And there shall be silence in heaven for the space of half an hour; and immediately after shall the curtain of heaven be unfolded, as a scroll is unfolded after it is rolled up, and the face of the Lord shall be unveiled.

At this point after the half hour of silence in heaven, the judgment is set and the reigns are turned over to the Lord as He prepares to destroy the wicked.

> And *the saints that are upon the earth, who are alive, shall be quickened and be caught up to meet him.*
>
> And they *who have slept in their graves shall come forth,* for their graves shall be opened; and *they also shall be caught up to meet him* in the midst of the pillar of heaven—
>
> They are Christ's, the first fruits, they who shall descend with him first, and they who are on the earth and in their graves, who are first caught up to meet him; and all this by the voice of the sounding of the trump of the angel of God.
>
> And after this another angel shall sound, which is the second trump; and *then cometh the redemption of those who are Christ's at his*

coming; who have received their part in that prison which is prepared for them, that they might receive the gospel, and *be judged* according to men in the flesh.

And again, another trump shall sound, which is the third trump; and then come *the spirits of men who are to be judged*, and are found under condemnation;

And these are the rest of the dead; and they live not again until the thousand years are ended, neither again, until the end of the earth. (D&C 88:95–101)

Revelation also records that, after the judgment begins, "them which destroy the earth" (Revelation 11:18) are to be destroyed. There will be a mighty earthquake and great hail, the winepress trodden down, and the earth reaped.

The timing of this gathering is precise and calculated. It comes at a time when the world celebrates its victory over the death of the two prophets in Jerusalem and subsequently witnesses their surprising resurrection. Heaven then declares an end to all kingdoms and that judgment is to be enacted upon "those which destroy the earth." With heaven declaring an end to all earthly kingdoms, the keys of the dispensations will be turned over to the Savior, and the judgment can take place.

To the world, this seems like another day in the chaotic reign of the beast. Then immediately, swift retribution comes as the mightiest earthquake in the history of the planet destroys the great Babylon in one hour, followed by great hail where each hailstone weighs a talent (see Revelation 16:20–21). The Lord then commands the waters to recede into the north, a highway is cast up out of the great deep, and the lost tribes return (see D&C 133:22–23).

The New Jerusalem

The New Jerusalem is a reference to two cities. Though the Jerusalem of old will also be rebuilt, it is not referred to as the "New Jerusalem."

And he spake also concerning the house of Israel, and *the Jerusalem from whence Lehi should come*—after it should be destroyed it should be built up again, a holy city unto the Lord; wherefore, it *could not be a new Jerusalem* for it had been in a time of old; but it should be built up again, and become a holy city of the Lord; and it should be built unto the house of Israel—

And that a *New Jerusalem should be built up upon this land*, unto the remnant of the seed of Joseph, for which things there has been a type. (Ether 13:5–6)

The first reference is to the New Jerusalem, which will also be known as Zion, which will be built in Jackson County, Missouri.

The second reference is to the holy city that will come down from heaven, which is also referred to as the "New Jerusalem." The holy city that comes down from heaven takes place after the Millennium, once the earth has been renewed.

And I saw a new heaven and a new earth: for the first heaven and the first earth were passed away; and there was no more sea.

And *I John saw the holy city, new Jerusalem, coming down from God out of heaven*, prepared as a bride adorned for her husband. (Revelation 21:1–2)

Revelation 21 goes on to give a brief description of the glory and magnificence of this heavenly city prepared of God.

From what we have read in Ether, we understand that the old Jerusalem will be rebuilt, and the building of a New Jerusalem on the American continent will take place. The timing of the rebuilding of Jerusalem is not clear; however, the building of Zion will begin prior to the Second Coming.

And the Lord said unto Enoch: As I live, even so will I come in the last days, in the days of wickedness and vengeance, to fulfil the oath which I have made unto you concerning the children of Noah;

And the day shall come that the earth shall rest, but before that day the heavens shall be darkened, and a veil of darkness shall cover the earth; and the heavens shall shake, and also the earth; and great tribulations shall be among the children of men, but my people will I preserve;

And righteousness will I send down out of heaven; and truth will I send forth out of the earth, to bear testimony of mine Only Begotten; his resurrection from the dead; yea, and also the resurrection of all men; and righteousness and truth will I cause to sweep the earth as with a flood, *to gather out mine elect from the four quarters of the earth, unto a place which I shall prepare, an Holy City, that my people may gird up their loins, and be looking forth for the time of my coming;* for there shall be my tabernacle, and it shall be called Zion, a New Jerusalem. (Moses 7:60–62)

One of the reasons for this is that when the Lord comes, He will bring the lands together. As the landmasses on this earth are reunited, the valleys will rise up, the mountains will be laid low, the waters will go into the north, and a highway will be cast up out of the great deep. We will see the greatest earthquake this planet has ever known. We can only begin to imagine what is going to be destroyed. The scriptures tell us that, in one hour, Babylon is completely destroyed.

Though some of the preparations for the New Jerusalem and the old Jerusalem may remain intact after this massive destruction, it is quite evident that there will be a lot of work to do once the Lord comes for there to be any holy cities during the Millennium.

In the case of the New Jerusalem in Jackson County, Missouri, we read,

And the Lord said unto Enoch: Then shalt thou and all thy city meet them there, and we will receive them into our bosom, and they shall see us; and we will fall upon their necks, and they shall fall upon our necks, and we will kiss each other;

And there shall be mine abode, and it shall be Zion, which shall come forth out of all the creations which I have made; and for the space of a thousand years the earth shall rest. (Moses 7:63–64)

The Saints will begin the building of the New Jerusalem, and then Enoch and his city will join them and become part of the New Jerusalem.

When we think upon the mission of the 144,000 or the opportunity to participate in the building of the New Jerusalem, it makes us proud to be a part of God's kingdom.

When we think upon the glorious reunion with the Savior at Adam-ondi-Ahman or welcoming the lost tribes, it thrills our souls. To be engaged in a righteous cause enlivens the spirit and gladdens the heart. Though the journey will require our most valiant efforts, the rewards will be great. However, these events are yet to come, and our task is to focus on today. We must look to the future to see where our path will lead. We must fight today's battles to prepare the way for tomorrow's challenges. What can we do today to prepare for tomorrow?

Summary Points

- The lost tribes are not part of the 144,000.
- The 144,000 high priests will be chosen from the remnant of those tribes who were led away.
- The lost tribes are not known to the world.
- The 144,000 will be comprised of those who are already known to the earth.
- Adam-ondi-Ahman will take place after the forty-two-month siege of Jerusalem, after heaven declares an end to all earthly kingdoms, and then after the two prophets in Jerusalem are resurrected.
- One of the grand purposes of Adam-ondi-Ahman is to turn the keys of the various dispensations back over to Christ.
- Adam-ondi-Ahman is, among other things, a reward to the Saints.
- The judgment will be begin at Adam-ondi-Ahman.
- The New Jerusalem will begin to be built prior to the Second Coming.
- Enoch and his city will join the New Jerusalem at the beginning of the millennial era.
- The old Jerusalem will be rebuilt as a holy city.

- After the Millennium, a celestialized New Jerusalem will then descend out of heaven to take up its place on the celestialized earth.

CHAPTER 6:
PREPARATIONS FOR OUR DAY

Physical Preparedness

To **be physically** prepared, we must know for what we are preparing. In our day, it will not be wars and rumors of wars, terrorist attacks, corruption, lawlessness, or economic strife that will be the events or the catalyst to change the world as we know it. All of these events will affect us, but they pale in comparison to what the scriptures tell us is next on the horizon: the worldwide earthquake in the sixth seal. This event will forever change our way of life on this planet. As the earth reels to and fro, there is, in addition to the obvious repercussions of a global event of this nature, the possibility of a pole shift, a change of the orbital pattern, or an alteration in the speed at which the earth spins on its axis.

We know that weather patterns will change and that at some point the Lord will release winds upon the face of the earth. These winds will cause difficulties in many ways, such as limiting travel or bringing adversity to daily living conditions such as gardening, agriculture, construction, ranching, manufacturing, and so on. If you combine the winds with the aftereffects of volcanic activity, causing the skies to be darkened and temperature decreases, it will mean that conventional methods of growing crops may have limited success. The need for food storage will be essential. In addition to food storage, we may have to know how to sprout beans or lentils and use other techniques to produce food crops under these adverse conditions.

Tsunamis and the seas heaving themselves beyond their bounds will be responsible for much devastation. Coastlines will change, some smaller countries may disappear, and the destruction of the many nuclear power facilities located near the oceans will likely result in radioactive contamination of global proportions.

On the continents, homes, businesses, roadways, utilities, factories, and so on will suffer varying degrees of damage. The entire globe will be under disaster conditions. There will be little to no relief available, other than what we can provide ourselves. Governments will fail. Political alliances will change. Laws will be disrespected as many use this crisis, when there will be little or no policing, as an opportunity to steal, loot, rape, murder, and commit wickedness. People will be more prone to engage in these activities when they think that they will not be caught or that they can escape accountability.

Electrical power could be interrupted for extended periods. We will not have access to the conveniences of items such as food, clothing, toilet paper, medicine, and medical supplies.

Gasoline and other fuels will be in short supply. Many roadways will have limited access. Banking systems will fail. (Certainly insurance companies will not be able to cover the losses.) Borders will go unprotected, and other events will cause problems for many communities. Food shortages, lack of shelter and clothing, and other losses will likely cause rioting and death.

We will have to cope with loss on many levels, including the deaths of family members. Many will think that this is the Second

Coming, and when the Lord does not come they will lose faith or make bad choices. Persecutions will increase, and society will continue to degrade.

These events will define us. Sacrifice should change our selfishness to selflessness, and serving others should increase our love for one other and our desire to live the commandments. Our true natures will be made manifest. As we adjust, we will have to cherish our religion to find peace and protection in this changed world. From this point on, wickedness will increase on the earth.

Now that some of the potential conditions emanating from this event have been discussed, what are some of the things that we can do to physically prepare for such an event? We have received counsel from prophets, past and present, on being prepared.

Have we followed their advice? Now that we understand the nature of what lies ahead, we can prepare as we feel prompted by the Spirit.

Here are some basic preparation ideas that may be geared toward this event.

- Preparations for home-food production: store up non-GMO seeds, purchase a book on how to harvest seeds and planting techniques, and acquire information on methods of nonconventional food production (sprouting and such).
- Create a library of written information on topics you feel may be of value. (The Internet will likely not be available. You can store all this in a five-gallon bucket with a lid.)
- Increase your working knowledge (and supplies) of first aid and medicine, including knowledge and storage of herbs or essential oils and other home remedies. Given the circumstances, we should have something to counteract the effects of radioactive contamination, such as nascent iodine, diatomaceous earth, and so on.
- Store tools, equipment, and supplies that may assist you in such circumstances. (Consider loss of electricity and heat, plastic for broken windows, water purification, and so on.)

The list is endless, and the purpose of this book is not to be an emergency resource manual. Hopefully these suggestions have simply given you an idea of where to begin.

Spiritual Preparedness

First, we must be living righteously and following the admonitions of the prophet. The Book of Mormon and other books of scripture admonish us to be awake to the world around us, to seek the Lord, and to have knowledge of and a communication with Him. We are to gain, by revelation, a testimony of these times, including an understanding of the unfolding of God's work to be prepared against the times. The blessings or fruits of righteous living will enable us to be humble enough to receive the promptings that God has for us.

If we are informed, we can ask the right questions and receive answers to our queries.

> And I give unto you *a commandment that you shall teach one another* the doctrine of the kingdom.
>
> Teach ye diligently and my grace shall attend you, that *you may be instructed more perfectly* in theory, in principle, in doctrine, in the law of the gospel, *in all things that pertain unto the kingdom of God, that are expedient for you to understand;*
>
> *Of things* both *in heaven and in the earth,* and *under the earth;* things *which have been,* things *which are,* things *which must shortly come to pass;* things *which are at home,* things *which are abroad;* the *wars and the perplexities of the nations, and the judgments which are on the land; and a knowledge also of countries and of kingdoms.* (D&C 88:77–79)

The Lord is clear in His desire to have the Saints be instructed in all things pertaining to the kingdom of God that are expedient for us to understand. Though we are taught some of this information at general conference, it is our responsibility to become more perfect in our knowledge of the principles, doctrines, and laws of the gospel. As this occurs, we can apply this knowledge to understand the past, present, and future of this world. It is important to understand that through diligent study and prayer, God's grace will attend us, and we will be enlightened in the following manner:

- We will understand where God stands in opposition to these things and where we should stand.
- We will be prepared to politically oppose these evils.
- We will be prepared to take action in our homes and communities against the onslaught of evil.
- We will understand the times and be prepared with food storage and other essentials.
- We will be prepared to stand in holy places (being worthy of and attending the temple).

Through this process of enlightenment, we will see more clearly the world that we live in and understand what role our Heavenly Father would like us to play in bringing forth the cause of truth and preparing for the Second Coming. As we become spiritually enlightened, we will understand that as we approach the Second Coming, the Lord has different requirements of us than He did of the Saints even five years ago. As we look around us, we can see that the Lord is hastening His work.

Now more than ever, there is a need for the Saints to study and understand the judgments that are upon the land. Having done this, we will be in a state of preparation, ready to ask the right questions and be directed of the Lord.

Prior to the Flood, Noah had to make preparations. Prior to traveling, we make preparations. Prior to the Second Coming, what are the preparations that we are required to make? Without being spiritually aware, we cannot know of these preparations, nor are we likely to make them.

Judgments upon the Land

As previously stated in Doctrine and Covenants 88:79, the Lord would like us to be aware, to study, and to know why there are judgments upon the land. If we listen carefully, we will hear the things we need to do, as Saints, from our leaders. Our obligation to the Lord is to avoid participating in the activities that are displeasing to Him and engage in the correct activities so that these judgments do not fall upon us. In other words, we need to be part of the solution and *not* part of the problem.

Mankind has always had the ability to choose to obey God's law. However, when we see moral decay, idolatry, greed, devil worship, corruption, and other gross and insidious crimes becoming more and more commonplace (and being supported by law), then we can expect heavenly retribution. The degree to which sin exists in our day is abominable.

God's laws are being challenged on just about every level. There are many excuses for deviating from the commandments. Many individuals claim that they are just acting according to the law or that they are not really hurting anyone.

Another common excuse is that they are simply exercising their freedom to choose, thus extricating themselves from any moral code. In the case of morality issues, the excuse that we often hear is that we have evolved socially and have a new morality. As the world pushes these agendas forward, they pass more and more laws to hedge up the way of righteousness.

King Mosiah's warnings of the difficulty in dealing with unrighteous kings illustrates how challenging it is to restore righteousness once wickedness becomes law and is upheld by alliances with those in power.

> And behold, now I say unto you, ye cannot dethrone an iniquitous king save it be through much contention, and the shedding of much blood.
>
> For behold, he has his friends in iniquity, and he keepeth his guards about him; and he teareth up the laws of those who have reigned in righteousness before him; and he trampleth under his feet the commandments of God;
>
> And he enacteth laws, and sendeth them forth among his people, yea, laws after the manner of his own wickedness; and whosoever

doth not obey his laws he causeth to be destroyed; and whosoever doth rebel against him he will send his armies against them to war, and if he can he will destroy them; and thus an unrighteous king doth pervert the ways of all righteousness.

And now behold I say unto you, it is not expedient that such abominations should come upon you. (Mosiah 29:21–24)

By having laws that permit sinful practices, society sends the message that sin is lawful, acceptable, and appropriate. Whether it is the right of homosexual marriage, legalized prostitution, or pornography in all of its forms, the forces of evil know no bounds. It is difficult for political representatives when lawmakers present, say, eight-five pages of good law, ten pages of mostly good law, and five pages of bad law to be passed as one bill. Society's influence is not limited to legislation.

Religion is becoming passé. Prayer is not allowed in public school, as it might offend someone. Sunday is no longer a sacred day—it is a holiday, with sporting events, barbeques, hiking, swimming, shopping, pleasure cruises, and so on. The motives for these changes are always the same: money, selfishness, thrills, greed, power, and self-gratification.

As we are exposed to wickedness, we become more tolerant; it affects us less, and we begin to allow certain behaviors that we would not have previously permitted. Listen to how Laman and Lemuel attempt to justify the behavior of the wicked Jews in their day.

And *we know that the people who were in the land of Jerusalem were a righteous people*; for they kept the statutes and judgments of the Lord, and all his commandments, according to the law of Moses; wherefore, we know that they are a righteous people; and *our father hath judged them*, and hath led us away because we would hearken unto his words; yea, and our brother is like unto him. And after this manner of language did my brethren murmur and complain against us. (1 Nephi 17:22)

At what point does compromise become sin? At what point does action or inaction cause judgments to come upon the land? As we examine this subject, there are many things that may give us pause, as we reevaluate our lives.

> Wo unto them that call evil good, and good evil, that put darkness for light, and light for darkness, that put bitter for sweet, and sweet for bitter. (2 Nephi 15:20)

Like the analogy of the frog in the pot, as the adversary slowly turns up the heat, we can fail to notice a temperature change until we are calling evil good and good evil. We often let society dictate our standards instead of dictating our standards to society. Instead of leading the charge for just causes, do we follow the flow of society, saying, "Oh well, what could we have done?" If it is justified according to the law, do we fail to use God's wisdom and instead act in mankind's wisdom, saying we have done no wrong?

The Lord has asked us to pray over everything that we do so that we can receive His guidance, wisdom, and direction in all that we do.

The scriptures tell us of the moral conditions that will exist in these last days, even among some of the Saints. The state of wickedness will continue to increase after the worldwide earthquake in the sixth seal, and we will see the Spirit slowly taken from the earth, as previously indicated by the prophet Joseph Fielding Smith. Thus the abomination of desolation will come upon us.

> And from the time that the daily sacrifice shall be taken away, and the abomination that maketh desolate set up, there shall be a thousand two hundred and ninety days. (Daniel 12:11)

> Verily, verily, I say unto you, darkness covereth the earth, and gross darkness the minds of the people, and all flesh has become corrupt before my face.
>
> Behold, vengeance cometh speedily upon the inhabitants of the earth, a day of wrath, a day of burning, a day of desolation, of weeping, of mourning, and of lamentation; and as a whirlwind it shall come upon all the face of the earth, saith the Lord.
>
> And upon my house shall it begin, and from my house shall it go forth, saith the Lord;

First among those among you, saith the Lord, who have professed to know my name and have not known me, and have blasphemed against me in the midst of my house, saith the Lord. (D&C 112:23–26)

Here, the Lord makes it known that some of the Saints will have blasphemed against Him in His house and that the daily sacrifice, or the opportunity to repent, will be taken away. Once wickedness reigns, the day of wrath will come upon us.

Occasionally, God has to destroy evil to prepare the way for righteousness. This happened with the people in the time of Noah and with the Nephites several generations after the Crucifixion of Christ. The clearing required for the millennial era to be ushered in will be of a greater degree. As these wicked conditions increase, judgments will be poured out upon people proportionately.

And the love of men shall wax cold, and iniquity shall abound. (D&C 45:27)

It is at this point, when the worldwide earthquake happens in the sixth seal, that the stage will be set for an outpouring of wickedness in the world.

When the world is in utter chaos and reeling from global catastrophe and the Savior does not appear, many of the earth's inhabitants will lose their hope in Christ and begin to follow other paths. It is when the world believes that Christ will not come, or believes that He does not exist, that moral compasses will cease to operate. Then lawlessness will abound, and conditions will degrade until Satan has all power.

In our telestial world, mankind's agenda often does not include God. As a direct consequence, many of the choices made are in the interest of the adversary. An example of this that can be applied to our day is found in Ether. This is simply one of many such problems that we face.

And it came to pass that Riplakish did not do that which was right in the sight of the Lord, for he did have many wives and concubines, and did lay that upon men's shoulders which was grievous to be borne; yea, he did tax them with heavy taxes; and with the taxes he did build many spacious buildings. (Ether 10:5)

Riplakish used his position and influence to place burdens upon the people to satisfy his own greed and pleasures. The adversary delights in seeing people under duress, hoping they will break laws and come under condemnation.

I do not believe that in any other time in history were there as many different taxes as we have today. What governments have achieved in our day through national, state, and provincial debt; world-assistance agreements; and the like has added to the burden of taxation. Whether by means of direct or indirect tax, it is difficult to pay such ridiculous sums. When huge corporate bailouts are offered from empty coffers, the result is certain.

This is a problem that is felt around the world. Economies in many countries are failing or have failed. When economic crises grip a country, they affects social structure. Everyday problems are magnified and spill out in domestic violence, theft, robbery, and anger, just to name a few. If there is political instability, such events can trigger riots, mass crime, and even civil war. It is our responsibility to find ways to stop these individuals from causing undue burdens to come upon the people.

It is part of the devil's plan to have masters over individuals through indebtedness. Those who seek control through these means are plotting their own demises, as their master has no promise of salvation.

In these the last days, to help us on the right path in governing our lands, the Lord has inspired honest men to guard against these evils. The Declaration of Independence, an inspired document, has been a beacon to many nations and a blessing to countless individuals as the cause of liberty has gone forward in our day. However, as the evil designs of conspiring people continue to move forward as well, our freedoms are being systematically eroded. To make matters worse, we allow uninspired leaders to make laws and forge agreements that slowly compromise our freedoms under the guise of universal cooperation or the betterment of the nation, instead of standing firm on principles of freedom and justice. If we do not seek to remove these evils, are we under condemnation? To what degree are we responsible for bringing God's judgments upon this land?

We are warned about this in the book of Ether.

> And *whatsoever nation shall uphold such secret combinations*, to get power and gain, until they shall spread over the nation, behold, they *shall be destroyed*; for the Lord will not suffer that the blood of his saints, which shall be shed by them, shall always cry unto him from the ground for vengeance upon them and yet he avenge them not.
>
> Wherefore, O ye Gentiles, *it is wisdom in God that these things should be shown unto you*, that thereby ye may repent of your sins, and *suffer not that these murderous combinations shall get above you, which are built up to get power and gain*—and the work, yea, even the work of destruction come upon you, yea, even *the sword of the justice of the Eternal God shall fall upon you, to your overthrow and destruction if ye shall suffer these things to be.*
>
> Wherefore, *the Lord commandeth you, when ye shall see these things come among you that ye shall awake to a sense of your awful situation,* because of this secret combination which shall be among you; or wo be unto it, because of the blood of them who have been slain; for they cry from the dust for vengeance upon it, and also upon those who built it up.
>
> For it cometh to pass that *whoso buildeth it up seeketh to overthrow the freedom of all lands, nations, and countries; and it bringeth to pass the destruction of all people,* for *it is built up by the devil,* who is the father of all lies; even that same liar who beguiled our first parents, yea, even that same liar who hath caused man to commit murder from the beginning; who hath hardened the hearts of men that they have murdered the prophets, and stoned them, and cast them out from the beginning. (Ether 8:22–25)

In their desire to control the earth and its peoples, corrupt men and women, through the vehicles of governments, international associations, and secret societies, place themselves beyond the law to achieve their ends. They seek to corrupt the people and society to achieve their goals.

Many international organizations are designed to be beyond the reach of the people or, by extension, the nations. An elite few decide the activities of these organizations, while entire nations can be opposed. Some good can come from these organizations, but others have goals and objectives that are in opposition to God. As these various avenues are exploited in the pursuit of greed and power, we are seeing our world slowly crumbling around us.

The days of sitting on the fence will soon be a thing of the past. The enemy is upon us. How will we respond? How *should* we be responding?

There are certain conditions that lead to God's wrath coming upon the nations. In this time of great spiritual distress upon the earth, we can see the unfolding of these conditions as they increase in power and influence.

During the last forty-two-month period prior to the Second Coming, all of the conditions will be in place for the full measure of God's wrath and judgments—in consequence of these conditions—to be poured out until the earth is prepared for the coming of Christ.

Now we must ask the question: How does understanding the judgments on the land help us to understand the unfolding of God's work in the last days?

Through study and the grace of God, the following will come to pass: We will know "the things which must shortly come to pass" and in which seal we should expect them. By studying "the things which are at home" and "the things that are abroad," we will be prepared to act upon the points of enlightenment previously mentioned.

When we combine this information with having a "knowledge of countries and kingdoms" and an understanding of the "wars and the perplexities of the nations," we will be able to understand more fully the judgments upon the land. Finally, this knowledge will help us to survive these judgments and avoid the abomination of desolation that surely is coming (D&C 88:77–85).

Lulled into Carnal Security (Not Enough Oil in Your Lamp)

If we fail to awake to what is happening to us and around us, we are being gently rocked, giving us a false sense of security.

> And others *will he pacify, and lull them away into carnal security*, that they will say: All is well in Zion; yea, Zion prospereth, all is well— and thus the devil cheateth their souls, and leadeth them away carefully down to hell. (2 Nephi 28:21)

Carnal security means that, in a temporal, worldly way, we feel secure. How is it we can be led carefully down to hell in this manner? Let us examine the premise: "All is well in Zion; yea, Zion prospereth, all is well—and thus the devil cheateth their souls." Does this mean that we are comfortable, not having to work too hard, and following conveniences that allow us more time to pursue the pleasures of life? A life of ease can tend to be less spiritual and more temporal or worldly. We can then be caught up in a cycle of seeking worldly pleasures.

The adversary desires to lull us so that we are asleep and not aware of the judgments on the land, or our unwitting participation in his plan. We must consider that all things are spiritual unto our Father in Heaven. The adversary does not want us to live the commandments or to make any preparations for the upcoming trials.

If we are living comfortably in a society of convenience, we will not see the need to prepare, we will lose the skill to prepare, and we will not have the wherewithal to prepare, having given up the tools, space, and materials (and yes, perhaps even the monetary means).

There are many conveniences that we enjoy in today's world that will disappear in the event of a disaster. The challenges we will face in these last days are going to be the greatest in the history of our world. As we watch the continuing earthquakes, storms, and other disasters increase around us, they will become more and more commonplace. As economies continue to fail, it will be another difficult time in a season.

Then something of a more serious nature will happen, and this already fragile world will be plunged into chaos. Many of us will be unprepared, having been lulled to sleep. God sends forth the elements as a means of calling the world to repentance.

> *How oft have I called upon you* by the *mouth of my servants*, and by the *ministering of angels*, and by *mine own voice*, and by the voice of *thunderings*, and by the voice of *lightnings*, and by the voice of *tempests*, and by the voice of *earthquakes*, and great *hailstorms*, and by the voice of *famines* and *pestilences of every kind,* and by the great sound of a *trump*, and by the voice of *judgment*, and by the voice of *mercy* all the day long, and by the voice of *glory and honor* and the *riches of eternal life*, and would have saved you with an *everlasting salvation*, but *ye would not!* (D&C 43:25)

The world will look upon these calamities as a condition of nature, not as a force of God. The world will attempt to discredit the divine nature of God's works by claiming the natural order of science without a God. This is Satan's way of keeping the world from understanding the true nature of these calamities. We need to refocus our thinking and understand to see that there is a message in the increasing number of earthquakes, storms, floods, and other disasters. The message is: Repent and come unto the Lord.

Think of the many things we would miss if the flow of goods to the stores ever stopped. Among these items are food, clothing, fuel, oil, building materials, medical supplies, vehicles, and so on—in other words, almost everything vital for survival.

There are many difficulties that arise in today's world of mass production. Large monopolies and buying groups control conditions of production and market trends. The problem that arises, especially in grain farming, is that genetically altered products are designed to be sterile so that people are required to purchase new seed every year.

With a firm lock on the original heritage stock, seed companies have grain farmers at their mercy. Most of the genetically altered seeds for vegetable production are able to reproduce for several years before sterility is an issue.

It is disconcerting to observe the degree to which large companies influence lawmakers. In the United States, there are several states that have laws governing simple gardens and to whom you are allowed to give your produce. This is an example of individual rights being quashed under the guise of protecting the public from the potential "dangers" of nonregulated home gardens. Grain farmers will be in a tough spot when seeds are not available because of a natural disaster.

Societies of ease are causing many other problems. The increasing quantity of prepared food that comes to us by whatever means is a sign of our inability to provide for ourselves, which often dictates our unhealthy lifestyles. Even if we set aside the health issues, we are still faced with a huge self-reliance problem. Here is an example of how we have been forewarned:

> Shortly after World War II, I was called by the First Presidency to go to Europe to reestablish our missions and set up a program for the distribution of food and clothing to the Saints. . . . These people were, of course, willing to barter practically anything for that commodity which sustains life—food.
>
> An almost forgotten means of economic self-reliance is the home production of food. We are too accustomed to going to stores and purchasing what we need. By producing some of our food we reduce, to a great extent, the impact of inflation on our money. More importantly, we learn how to produce our own food and involve all family members in a beneficial project. No more timely counsel, I feel, has been given by President Kimball than his repeated emphasis to grow our own gardens. Here is one sample of his emphasis over the past seven years:
>
> "We encourage you to grow all the food that you feasibly can on your own property. Berry bushes, grapevines, fruit trees—plant them if your climate is right for their growth. Grow vegetables and eat them from your own yard."

Many of you have listened and done as President Kimball coun-
seled, and you have been blessed for it. Others have rationalized
that they had no time or space. . . . We encourage you to be more
self-reliant so that, as the Lord has declared, "notwithstanding the
tribulation which shall descend upon you, . . . the church may stand
independent above all other creatures beneath the celestial world"
(D&C 78:14). The Lord wants us to be independent and self-reliant
because these will be days of tribulation. He has warned and forewarned us of the eventuality. (Ezra Taft Benson, "Prepare for the Days
of Tribulation," *Ensign*, November 1980)

We need to be aware of what is going on around us. We must
ask ourselves, "What should I be doing about it?" We have been
given counsel. Have we been following that counsel, or are we being
lulled into carnal security? As a people and as individuals, if we do
not have our storage, if we do not have our plans, and if we do not
have essential information and means, then we are not prepared and
have not followed the commandments.

What kind of oil should you put in your lamp? Oil for lamps is
composed of scripture study, wheat, service, vegetable seeds, temple
work, water purification supplies, home teaching, beans and lentils,
prayer, power generators, political involvement, missionary work,
community assistance, family home evening, gardening, genealogy, hunting and fishing supplies, journals, military preparedness,
fasting and prayer, medical supplies, love, warning your neighbor,
keeping the commandments, and being charitable, to name a few.
If you top all this off with following your leaders and keeping the
Spirit as your guide, you will be ready.

Our duty in this regard is not to be slothful servants. We are not
to depend on our neighbors' preparedness or assume that someone
in the ward or stake will help us. Remember that the five wise
virgins told the others to go and buy from those that sell. This does
not preclude us from sharing; however, we cannot expect that others
should be required to prepare on our behalf.

Ultimately, the responsibility falls upon each of us to fill our own
lamps with oil. Remember, it takes time to prepare. The Lord will

bless us after we have done all that we are able. If you look carefully at the suggested list of items of which oil for lamps should be composed, you will notice that not all of the items can be purchased.

When Ezra Taft Benson said that "the revelation to produce and store food may be as essential to our temporal welfare today as boarding the ark was to the people in the days of Noah" (Ezra Taft Benson, "Prepare for the Days of Tribulation"), he was not just making a suggestion. He meant it.

For example, if there were a situation, like a worldwide earthquake, where you needed food but could not produce it and did not have enough of it because you did not listen to counsel, and there is no one around to help you, and you die, it is not because God does not love you.

To understand what the Lord would have you do, you must be specific in your petitions. As individuals, we cannot hope to be prepared if we do not ask with a sincere heart.

The natural man offends God. As we prepare for the Second Coming, we will be required to live more righteously. We need put off the natural man. As we do this, we will have a greater portion of the Spirit and will receive the direction and help we require. We will need the seal of God.

As the corruption in the world increases, so do the distractions to keep us from dedicating time and resources to properly preparing. There is always a new movie or new fashions or new video games. The list goes on. With church and family thrown in the mix, who has time to become involved in the future? After all, someone on the ward or stake level will let us know. The prophet or the Brethren should say something, should they not?

Meaning Well and Doing Well

We have been given counsel in the area of preparedness many times. In these last days, this counsel has not changed. If you ask a Latter-day Saint about the law of chastity, they will know the answer. If you ask them about food storage, they will know the answer. The

Church has fulfilled its responsibility in this matter. As we see the increased need for preparation, we should be acting in accordance without someone to hold our hand.

In the case of emergency preparedness, many prophets have encouraged us to do something every week so that eventually we will be prepared. In the case of moral and political issues, it becomes our responsibility to bring to pass good works of our own accord. The majority of the time, it is the voice of a few who promote evil. There are still many good people who will stand behind a good cause.

But in the absence of a group of people standing up for right, people have a tendency to shrug their shoulders and say, "What is the use?" The worse corruption gets, the harder it becomes to fight against it. Does this mean that, even if evil will be temporarily successful, we are not required to stand for truth?

> "All that is necessary for evil to triumph is for good men to do nothing."
> (Attributed to Edmund Burke; no definite original source.)

We must do everything in our power to protect our freedoms and liberties. What are our obligations? In our efforts to stand for truth, we should exercise our will to follow God, strengthen our testimonies, and be actively engaged in bringing to pass good works. In so doing, we will receive the inspiration that comes from God to those who are doing all they can.

We should be pursuing every honest means to set at naught the advances of evil and designing individuals. We need to stand firm against the slippery and sly means that are employed to twist the commandments.

We must be aware of the ever-so-slight relaxing of our grip on the truth. The commandments of God have not changed, nor have His truths. The world is changing rapidly, and the time is at hand when the Saints of God will be persecuted and hated. Many challenges lie ahead as we try to defend righteousness.

The intention of the adversary is to cause insurrection, economic upheaval, war, hatred, and so on, and he will use any means to achieve his goals. From this point forward, the world will continue to degenerate as we approach the Second Coming. We must increase in righteousness to receive the blessings of safety and prosperity that will enable us to be preserved from the judgments that are coming.

We need to evaluate our situations and decide if we need new laws in our communities. If we implement local laws, it will act as a precedent and be seen as the will of the people. In this way, we can oppose state, provincial, or federal laws that seek to set aside or throw down justice. This will at least give us a legal means to stand against unscrupulous political forces.

In preparing for times of tribulation, do we need to bring our community laws in line with the needs of these times to allow easy and affordable means for people to gather to our communities? Are we doing everything within our power to ease the burden of taxation? Do we really have the interests of other people at heart? What are our plans in the event of economic failure, electrical failure, or loss of heat? What are our plans for communications failure, or the lack of goods and services? Are our communities self-sufficient?

We need to determine in what manner we ought to be prepared. Captain Moroni used the wisdom of God to change the defense strategies of his time. It is time for us to seek God's wisdom in preparing for these things that will come upon us.

Perhaps it is time to put away the golf clubs, postpone the cruises, sell the unnecessary luxuries, and prepare as best we can at this late hour.

Concluding Remarks

As we understand the significance of the approaching events, we can use this information to make sound choices. It only makes sense that the degree to which we are physically and spiritually prepared within our means will be a reflection of the degree to which our Heavenly Father can assist us. As we understand more fully the unfolding of God's work in these last days, we can make better preparations to help us. Though we do not know the time when these events will happen, we should realize that having been given the knowledge we have, it becomes our responsibility to prepare and to warn our neighbors.

For those who seek wisdom, the Lord reveals His mysteries that they may be the means of doing much good. In return, the Lord rewards those who earnestly seek after Him.

> *Seek not for riches but for wisdom*, and behold, *the mysteries of God shall be unfolded unto you*, and then shall you be made rich. Behold, he that hath eternal life is rich.
>
> Verily, verily, I say unto you, *even as you desire of me so it shall be unto you; and if you desire, you shall be the means of doing much good* in this generation. (D&C 6:7–8)

Alma teaches his son that to gain information from God, he must inquire diligently of Him, and then He will reveal His mysteries to him. Nephi gives this same counsel.

> Behold, he bringeth to pass the resurrection of the dead. But behold, my son, the resurrection is not yet. Now, I unfold unto you a mystery; nevertheless, there are many mysteries which are kept, that no one knoweth them save God himself. But I show unto you one thing which *I have inquired diligently of God that I might know*—that is concerning the resurrection. (Alma 40:3)

> For *he that diligently seeketh shall find; and the mysteries of God shall be unfolded unto them, by the power of the Holy Ghost*, as well in these times as in times of old, and as well in times of old as in times to come; wherefore, the course of the Lord is one eternal round. (1 Nephi 10:19)

The message of the book of Revelation is plain. It recounts the plan of salvation, our eternal origins, our life here on earth, and the results of our choices. God's judgments are going to be poured out upon mankind. The words of Revelation have been given to us in a detailed and descriptive manner. Are we listening?

There was a war in heaven. That war is still raging. This is how it will end. Be prepared. The Lord will watch over the righteous, and He will return.

It is my prayer that those who read this book might diligently seek God's wisdom and thereby become the means of doing much good. May God bless you in your righteous endeavors.

Worldwide Earthquake (every island and every mountain moved out of it's place).

Four Winds Released by Angels (to hurt the earth, the sea, and the trees).

The Half Hour of Silence in Heaven (an approximate period of time +/- 20.83 earth years; how much more or how much less we are not sure).

Time, Times, and Half a Time (the last 42 month period prior to the second coming of Christ; this is also a part of the half hour of silence in heaven).

TRUMPETS

1. Fire and hail mingled with blood (1/3 trees and green grass burned).
2. Great mountain burning with fire cast into the sea (1/3 ships and sea life destroyed).
3. Great star falls from Heaven ("wormwood"; makes waters bitter).
4. Sun, moon, and stars smitten (no light 1/3 of the time).
5. Bottomless pit opened (locusts with power of scorpions).
6. Angels in Euphrates released to kill 1/3 of men.

VIALS

1. Evil, grievous sore.
2. Sea becomes as blood.
3. Rivers and fountains become as blood.
4. Men scorched with heat and burned.
5. Darkness and pains.
6. Euphrates dried up.

TRUMPET 7 VIAL 7

World's greatest earthquake (islands flee, mountains not found, continents come together), great hail (hail stones average 76 lbs.), water commanded into the North, highway cast up out of the deep, Mount of Olives split in two, righteous saints caught up to meet Christ, day of burning, Satan's earthly kingdom is destroyed.

The Unfolding of God's Work in the Last Days

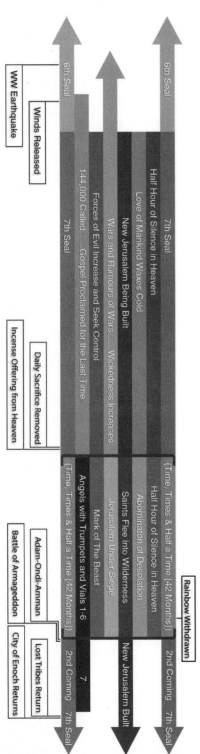

WW Earthquake

Winds Released

6th Seal

7th Seal

6th Seal

7th Seal
Half Hour of Silence in Heaven
Love of Mankind Waxes Cold
New Jerusalem Being Built
Wars and Rumours of Wars...... Wickedness Increases
Forces of Evil Increase and Seek Control
144,000 Called...... Gospel Proclaimed for the Last Time

Incense Offering from Heaven

Daily Sacrifice Removed

Rainbow Withdrawn

(Time, Times & Half a Time [42 Months])
Half Hour of Silence in Heaven
Abomination of Desolation
Saints Flee Into Wilderness
Jerusalem Under Siege
Mark of The Beast
Angels with Trumpets and Vials 1-6
(Time, Times & Half a Time [42 Months])

Battle of Armageddon

Adam-Ondi-Ahman

Lost Tribes Return

City of Enoch Returns

2nd Coming   7th Seal

7

2nd Coming   7th Seal

New Jerusalem Built

151

SOURCES

Jack Finegan, *Handbook of Biblical Chronology: Principles of Time Reckoning in the Ancient World and Problems of Chronology in the Bible* (Princeton: Princeton University Press, 1964).

John Heinerman, *Joseph Smith and Herbal Medicine* (Springville, Utah: Bonneville Books, 2007).

Lynn M. Hilton, *The Kolob Theorem A Mormon's View of God's Starry Universe* (Lindon, Utah: Granite Publishing and Distribution, May 2006).

Holy Bible, Authorized King James Version (Salt Lake City: The Church of Jesus Christ of Latter-day Saints, 1979).

Joseph Smith's "New Translation" of the Bible (Independence, Missouri: Herald, 1970).

Latter-day Prophets and the Doctrine and Covenants, comp. Roy W. Doxey (Salt Lake City: Deseret Book, 1978).

Bruce R. McConkie, *Mormon Doctrine*, Second Edition (Salt Lake City: Bookcraft, 1979).

Bruce R. McConkie, *Doctrinal New Testament Commentary*, 3 vols. (Salt Lake City: Bookcraft, 1965–73).

Donald W. Parry and Jay A. Parry, *Understanding the Book of Revelation* (Salt Lake City: Deseret Book, 1998).

David J. Ridges, *65 Signs of the Times Leading up to the Second Coming* (Springville, Utah: Cedar Fort, Inc., 2009).

David J. Ridges, *Your Study of the New Testament Made Easier* (Springville, Utah: Cedar Fort, Inc., 2007).

Joseph Smith, *History of The Church of Jesus Christ of Latter-day Saints*, 7 vols. (Salt Lake City: The Church of Jesus Christ of Latter-day Saints, 1932–51).

Joseph Smith, *Teachings of the Prophet Joseph Smith*, comp. Joseph F. Smith (Salt Lake City: Deseret Book, 1976).

Joseph Fielding Smith, *Signs of the Times: A Series of Discussions* (Salt Lake City: Deseret News, 1942).

Joseph Fielding Smith, *The Way to Perfection: Short Discourses on Gospel Themes* (Salt Lake City: Genealogical Society of Utah, 1931).

Joseph Fielding Smith, *Essentials in Church History: A History of the Church From the Birth of Joseph Smith Until the Present Time* (Salt Lake City: Deseret News, 1922).

Joseph Fielding Smith, *Doctrines of Salvation: Sermons and Writings of Joseph Fielding Smith*, comp. Bruce R. McConkie (Salt Lake City: Bookcraft, 1954–56).

Joseph Fielding Smith, *Answers to Gospel Questions* (Salt Lake City: Bookcraft, 1957–66).

The Book of Mormon (Salt Lake City: The Church of Jesus Christ of Latter-day Saints, 1981).

The Doctrine and Covenants (Salt Lake City: The Church of Jesus Christ of Latter-day Saints, 1981).

The Pearl of Great Price (Salt Lake City: The Church of Jesus Christ of Latter-day Saints, 1981).

Brigham Young, *Discourses of Brigham Young*, sel. John A. Widtsoe (Salt Lake City: Deseret Book, 1941).

Articles

Ezra Taft Benson, "Prepare for the Days of Tribulation," *Ensign*, November 1980.

Rudger J. Clawson, in Conference Report, October 1913, 59.

Jihong Cole-Dai, Ellen Mosley-Thompson, Shawn P. Wight, and Lonnie G. Thompson, "A 4,100-year record of explosive volcanism from an East Antarctica ice core," *Journal of Geophysical Research*, Vol. 105, No. D19 (October 16, 2000).

Kate Lunau, "Look Out Below," *Maclean's Magazine*, June 25, 2009.

Bruce R. McConkie, "Understanding the Book of Revelation," *Ensign*, September 1975.

NASA Science, "Solar Superstorm," *Science News*, October 23, 2003.

Richard B. Stothers, "The Great Tambora Eruption in 1815 and Its Aftermath," *Science* 224 (1984).

Richard B. Stothers and Michael R. Rampino, "Volcanic eruptions in the Mediterranean before A.D. 630 from written and archaeological sources," *Journal of Geophysical Research*, August 10, 1983.

Dieter, F. Uchtdorf, "Two Principles for Any Economy," *Ensign*, November 2009.

Matt Williams, "A Red Moon—Not a Sign of Apocalypse," *Universe Today*, November 1, 2014.

ABOUT THE AUTHOR

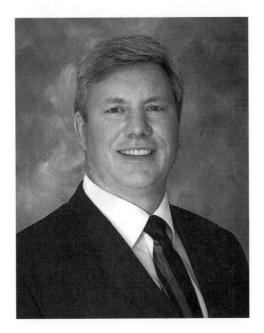

*G**regory A. Ranger*** was born and raised in the foothills of the Canadian Rockies, where he grew to love the wonders of God's creations through Scouting, hunting, and fishing. Greg is an avid student of the gospel, an experienced tradesman, and a university graduate. He believes that it is when we effectively apply our life's experience that we put ourselves in a position to succeed. The pursuit of gospel knowledge is just one example. "We can ponder the scriptures; look for practical explanations; pray for God's enlightenment and go forward with confidence to find the answers." The path is not always easy, but the journey can have great rewards. Greg and his wife, Dawn, are the parents of six children and reside in southern Alberta.

SCAN to visit

WWW.GREGORYRANGERAUTHOR.COM